F E (Frank Ernest) Halliday, the literary scholar and Cornwall historian, was born in Bradford, Yorkshire, on February 10, 1903.

Author of numerous books on Shakespeare, and English and Cornish history, one of his favourite writers was Thomas Hardy.

Halliday was educated at Bradford Grammar School, Giggleswick School and King's College, Cambridge, where he read economics for two years, taking tutorials with Keynes, until deciding to switch to English. He married Nancibel Gaunt in 1927, and they had one son, Sebastian. Halliday taught English and history at Cheltenham College from 1929 to 1947, when the family moved to St Ives, in Cornwall, where Halliday remained for the rest of his life.

Halliday's first book was published in 1946. He produced another twenty-three books, his last being published in 1975.

Now, twenty-five years since the publication of his last book, there is a renewed interest in Halliday. There are plans for an F E Halliday archive at the Archive Study Centre in Cornwall – which has its own website – and there are some fifty references to his work on the Internet.

Halliday died in 1982.

BY THE SAME AUTHOR
ALL PUBLISHED BY HOUSE OF STRATUS

CHAUCER AND HIS WORLD
DOCTOR JOHNSON AND HIS WORLD
A HISTORY OF CORNWALL
THE LIFE OF SHAKESPEARE
ROBERT BROWNING: HIS LIFE AND WORK
SHAKESPEARE AND HIS CRITICS
A SHAKESPEARE COMPANION
SHAKESPEARE IN HIS AGE
THOMAS HARDY: HIS LIFE AND WORK
UNFAMILIAR SHAKESPEARE
WORDSWORTH AND HIS WORLD

F E Halliday

The Poetry of Shakespeare's Plays

First published in 1954

Copyright © Sebastian Halliday

All rights reserved. No part of this publication may be reproduced, stored in a retrieval system, or transmitted, in any form, or by any means (electronic, mechanical, photocopying, recording, or otherwise), without the prior permission of the publisher. Any person who does any unauthorised act in relation to this publication may be liable to criminal prosecution and civil claims for damages.

The right of F E Halliday to be identified as the author of this work has been asserted.

This edition published in 2001 by House of Stratus, an imprint of
Stratus Holdings plc, 24c Old Burlington Street, London, W1X 1RL, UK.
Also at: Suite 210, 1270 Avenue of the Americas, New York, NY 10020, USA.

www.houseofstratus.com

Typeset, printed and bound by House of Stratus.

A catalogue record for this book is available from the British Library
and the Library of Congress.

ISBN 1-84232-125-0

This book is sold subject to the condition that it shall not be lent, resold, hired out, or otherwise circulated without the publisher's express prior consent in any form of binding, or cover, other than the original as herein published and without a similar condition being imposed on any subsequent purchaser, or bona fide possessor.

CONTENTS

Part One	*Introduction*	1
Part Two	Early Plays and Poems	59
	Chapter One: Histories *2 Henry VI, 3 Henry VI, Richard III, 1 Henry VI*	61
	Chapter Two: Poems *Venus and Adonis, The Rape of Lucrece*	71
	Chapter Three: Comedies *The Comedy of Errors, The Taming of the Shrew,* *The Two Gentlemen of Verona, (Titus Andronicus)*	81
Part Three	Sonnets and Lyrical Plays *Love's Labour's Lost, Romeo and Juliet, Richard II,* *A Midsummer Night's Dream, King John,* *The Merchant of Venice*	91
Part Four	Historical and Romantic Comedies *1 Henry IV, 2 Henry IV, Henry V,* *The Merry Wives of Windsor, Much Ado about Nothing,* *As You Like It, Twelfth Night*	131
Part Five	Tragedies of Character and Quasi-Romantic Comedies *Julius Caesar, Troilus and Cressida, Hamlet,* *All's Well that Ends Well, Measure for Measure, Othello,* *Macbeth, King Lear, Timon of Athens, Coriolanus,* *Antony and Cleopatra*	159
Part Six	Romances *Pericles, Cymbeline, The Winter's Tale, The Tempest*	215
Part Seven	Epilogue *Henry VIII, The Two Noble Kinsmen*	243

Part One

INTRODUCTION

Once a great artist has been securely settled upon his pedestal his work is sure to be misunderstood, for in the popular mind the peculiar quality of its greatness, if ever it has been fully appreciated, will soon be diminished or even obscured by other qualities thought to be inseparable from genius. Any misunderstanding about the genius of Shakespeare, however, must be attributed partly to the devotees originally responsible for his apotheosis, and curiously little has been done since then to correct it. The popular conception, or misconception, of Shakespeare is a confused and muddled affair made up of the fragments of criticism of three centuries; it is of a man comparatively uneducated, who yet contrived to be one of the most learned men of his age, a philosopher whose sententious maxims afford a daily guidance, the author of *Hamlet* and *The Merchant of Venice*, of Polonius' advice to Laertes, and Portia's speech on mercy, a dramatist with some reputation as a poet.

The idea that Shakespeare was an inspired peasant probably derives from Ben Jonson, but it was fixed like so many other standards that we accept today by the eighteenth century, and it was the critics of that age who imposed on posterity the concept of Shakespeare as philosopher and sage rather than as artist and poet. For Pope, Shakespeare's verse lacked lustre and polish, his plays were rambling and irregular structures, but his characters were Nature herself, and he himself a natural sage, a philosopher born. This conception of Shakespeare as a prophet-like figure has been visibly perpetuated in the statue by Scheemakers in

THE POETRY OF SHAKESPEARE'S PLAYS

Westminster Abbey, for the erection of which Pope was partly responsible. Johnson was even less susceptible to Shakespeare's poetry than Pope, whose judgment he applauded and emphatically confirmed, and for him Shakespeare was above all a masterly creator of character, and a writer of plays that are full of 'practical axioms and domestic wisdom' from which 'may be collected a system of civil and economical prudence'. The years between the erection of the Scheemakers' statue in 1740 and the publication of Johnson's *Preface* to his edition of Shakespeare in 1765 were precisely those of Garrick's popularization of the plays on the stage, either in the original or in 'improved' versions; in 1758 he commissioned the very thoughtful and gentlemanly statue by Roubillac, and in 1769 presided over the official apotheosis of Shakespeare at the Stratford Jubilee which he organized. After this, and until the beginning of the present century, the plays were the ideal medium for exhibiting the virtuosity of star actors, from the Kembles and Keans to Irving and Tree, and though they gradually abandoned the adaptations, their versions were progressively mutilated and distorted to make time for the irrelevancies of scenic illusion and the fripperies of heavily upholstered spectacle. The greatest glory of English art suffered the degradation that most great art has to endure, that of being wrenched out of its conventional form to fit into the mould of nature; a play must be made to look like the thing itself, a slice of life, and, if theatrical exigencies demand it, to sound like it as well.

This vulgarizing process was not allowed to pass without protest. Early in the nineteenth century Charles Lamb ridiculed the inscription under the 'harlequin figure' of Garrick in Westminster Abbey,[1] protested against the tyranny of the stage and the star actors, and pleaded for the fine abstraction of reading the plays as against the gross

INTRODUCTION

distraction of seeing a Kemble or Kean production, roundly declaring that the 'Lear of Shakespeare cannot be acted'. Hazlitt, too: 'We do not like to see our author's plays acted, and least of all *Hamlet*'; 'All that is finest in *A Midsummer Night's Dream* is lost in the presentation... Poetry and the stage do not agree well together.' 'Poetry'! Though Hazlitt's book was called *Characters of Shakespeare's Plays*, it was the first to consider, though only in a general way, the poetry of the plays, the first *book*, indeed, to recognize the poetry as a major element in the plays at all. Yet even Hazlitt thought of Shakespeare as 'mere poet', that is, as distinct from dramatic poet, inferior to Chaucer and Spenser. It remained for Coleridge to show that Shakespeare was a poet before he was a dramatic poet, and to refute Pope and Jonson by demonstrating that his judgment was equal to his genius, that the plays have an organic unity superior to the mechanical symmetry demanded by the eighteenth century.

These protests and discoveries had some practical effect, and Benjamin Webster, Samuel Phelps, William Poel and Frank Benson tried to stem the swelling stream of extravagant travesties by performing the full texts of all the plays with the minimum of apparatus, but Coleridge's thesis that Shakespeare was a great artist as well as a great genius encouraged the belief that all things were possible with him; the floods of exclamatory criticism and delirious adulation were loosed, and the Germans solemnly and massively joined in. Shakespeare was a great philosopher, scholar, soldier, lawyer, courtier, scientist, doctor, the most universal genius that had ever lived, and books on Shakespeare as this, on Shakespeare as that, on the major characters, the minor characters, the heroes, the heroines, and even on the girlhood of the heroines poured from the press. The Shakespeare Society, The New Shakespeare Society, and the Shakespeare-Gesellschaft were founded, and transactions and year books swelled the torrent of publications, augmented now by biographical studies and treatises on Shakespeare's theatre. Much of this was admirable and invaluable, but, though there was much ado about Shakespeare's verse, there was precious little ado about his poetry.

Small wonder that the ordinary man was bewildered by this welter of conflicting impressions: Shakespeare the Stratford rustic, Shakespeare the seer and savant, Shakespeare fair and bearded, Shakespeare dark and clean-shaven, as revealed in the newly discovered authentic likenesses, even, perhaps, Shakespeare as Sir Henry Irving or Sir Beerbohm Tree, and somehow associated with plush seats, and real grass and live rabbits. And small wonder that others rejected this inapprehensible protean figure, and were driven to look for the author of the plays and poems, not in the Warwickshire peasant but in Bacon or the Earls of Rutland, Derby or Oxford, or even in Queen Elizabeth. The twentieth century has done much to clear up the nineteenth-century muddle, by a more critical criticism, a more scholarly scholarship, and by a much more intelligent presentation of the plays, yet some of the confusion remains, and it is still possible for well-informed people to ask how an uneducated man like Shakespeare could possibly have written so much and so learnedly.

But there is no Shakespeare mystery, and no reason for confusion; nor was there anything abnormal in his life, about which research has revealed more than we had any right to expect. He was the son of a prosperous businessman who became bailiff, or mayor, of Stratford, and of a woman who was a member of one of the best families in Warwickshire. Almost certainly he had an excellent education at Stratford grammar school until he was sixteen, possibly served for a time in a lawyer's office; but he was a

INTRODUCTION

poet, and therefore went to London to earn a living as a writer of the new and popular poetic drama. By the time he was twenty-five or twenty-six his plays were being performed, and by the time he was thirty he was a member of the leading company of actors, the Lord Chamberlain's, and therefore well acquainted with the poets and wits, with the Inns of Court men, with the nobility and with the court. His plays were popular both in the public theatres and royal palaces, and his profession was sufficiently profitable to allow him to retire before he was fifty to the house that he had bought in Stratford. It is a story of success, but in no way remarkable; quite clear in its outlines, but inevitably obscure in detail, and easy therefore for those with a taste for such things to bedevil with mystery. After his death a monument was erected to him in Stratford church, and a collected edition of his plays published with a portrait, and this engraving and the bust of the monument, which resemble each other, must be accepted as the only authentic, though possibly not very accurate, likenesses.

It must be emphasized that Shakespeare was well educated; Stratford grammar school was one of the best in the country, and by the time he was sixteen the highly intelligent boy would have learned more than a smattering of Latin and other subjects, and once in London as an actor-dramatist with a reputable company he would be in constant contact and even companionship with many of the remarkable men of that very remarkable age. This was a far more liberal education than that of, say, a university man who settled as a parson in a provincial parish. On the other hand, it must as emphatically be affirmed that Shakespeare was not a learned man, a scholar, and there is nothing in his work to suggest that he was. There are a few Latin quotations in his early plays, not always over-accurate, and he had learned something of classical mythology at school;

he had no Greek, but some French and Italian he would pick up in London, and his eager and retentive mind would quickly grasp, both from his conversation with scholars, courtiers, travellers and other men of the world, and from his extensive reading, all the knowledge that is revealed in his works, which is remarkable only for its breadth and not for its profundity. When his authority, Holinshed or Plurarch for example, makes a mistake so does he, and his pages are full of topographical muddles and anachronisms. Not only was he not learned, in the sense that he was not a profound scholar, he was not even a profound thinker. He was an exceedingly intelligent, sensitive, well-balanced and witty man, full of a natural wisdom, but on examination most of the stock quotations will be found to be platitudes, and the favourite passages truisms, 'what oft was thought, but' – and this is the all-important thing – 'n'er so well expressed'. There is more originality and profundity of thought in a few of Bernard Shaw's best plays than in the whole of Shakespeare's works, as Shaw himself was the first disarmingly to admit. Finally, if anybody should ask how Shakespeare could have written so much, let him consider his contemporary, Thomas Heywood, who 'had either an entire hand or at the least a main finger' in two hundred and twenty plays.

That he should have written so well is another matter, but, though the twentieth century has sifted the deposits of the nineteenth, cleared away much of the rubbish, and itself contributed valuable material, disappointingly little has been done to emphasize and illuminate the sublimest quality of Shakespeare's genius, the poetry, though, indirectly almost, something has been achieved. The emphasis has been mainly on the theatre, on the physical structure of the Elizabethan playhouse, and its corollary, the presentation of the plays something after the manner in which they were

INTRODUCTION

originally produced, has led inevitably to a finer appreciation of the verse. Again, the interpretations of Granville-Barker and Mr Wilson Knight are largely in terms of the poetry, and the recent studies of the imagery draw attention to one element in it.[2] Finally, there have been a few essays treating generally, or of particular aspects of the poetry, and Dr Sitwell has recently published her *Notebook*.[3] But it is still insufficiently realized, indeed scarcely realized at all, by many people interested in the drama that Shakespeare was above all things a poet, that his plays contain, or rather are contained by, the greatest poetry that has been written in our language, perhaps the greatest that has been written in any language, and that it is in his poetry that he is almost divinely profound.

Most of the criticism has been on the old lines, on the characters of the plays, and on Shakespeare as dramatist. Of course Shakespeare is of all writers in English the supreme dramatist, and of all writers in the world the supreme creator of character, and had he never written a line of verse he would still have been so. That this is so is suggested by the fact that the seven historical and romantic comedies from *I Henry IV* to *Twelfth Night* contain far more prose than verse, while *The Merry Wives* is almost entirely in prose, and the most famous comic figure in literature, Falstaff, who dominates three of the plays, speaks only a dozen lines of verse. Yet – and this is the second point that I wish to make – Shakespeare is so far above all others as dramatist and creator of character because he is so far above all others as poet. A prose *Romeo and Juliet* or *Midsummer Night's Dream* or *Tempest* is scarcely conceivable, for the poetry *is* the play, while a prose *Hamlet*, *Othello*, *Lear*, *Macbeth* and *Antony and Cleopatra*, though conceivable, would be mere shadows of what they are, for the poetry is inseparable from the characters, the poetry *is* the character.

The Poetry of Shakespeare's Plays

Hamlet, Othello and the rest of the tragic heroes and heroines, and in a lesser degree the characters in the other plays, are what they are because of what they say, or rather because of how they say it, because of the poetry, and some of the tragic heroes, Macbeth and King John, for example, are tragic heroes at all only because of their poetry, without which they would be unable to retain our sympathy. It follows, then, that to write of Shakespeare's characters without relating them to their poetry is to write in a vacuum, and that the aesthetic criticism of Shakespeare's plays must begin with an appreciation of the poetry.

It follows also that the plays must be read, as we read the works of Milton or of any other non-dramatic poet. To hear in a theatre a Shakespearean play that we do not know almost by heart is to miss half its beauty, for not only do we miss the finer points of the poetry, but, unless we can afford the most expensive seats, we miss much of the poetry altogether. We go, or should go, to a Shakespearean play, not so much to see it, as to hear it, and we, that is the whole audience, shall never hear the whole of a Shakespearean play until we have a theatre resembling that for which it was written, with an apron stage projecting into the middle of the auditorium, on which the actors can speak unencumbered by canvas and undistracted by fancy lighting. The modern picture-frame stage is the product of a commercialized theatre and of a decadent drama that aims at the illusion of real life, and with its ingenious stage effects distressingly seductive to the producer; it is good enough for the majority of plays, the prose of which is not worth hearing for its own sake, and which lose little by occasional inaudibility, and admirable for a pantomime or a musical comedy, but it is a quite inadequate medium for the presentation of any play that depends primarily on its language, for the poetic drama, above all, therefore, for the

INTRODUCTION

plays of Shakespeare. They were written for performance without a break and with the minimum of apparatus, the action moving rhythmically and swiftly both in depth and on two levels, flowing from outer to inner and upper stages and back again to the platform, and in no other way can the forty-two scenes of *Antony and Cleopatra*, the supreme example of Shakespeare's stagecraft, be produced.[4] Fortunately we can see productions today under approximately these conditions at Stratford, the Old Vic, and other theatres where it is realized that Shakespeare did not write his plays to be performed bit by bit inside a picture-frame defined by footlights.

The plays, then, should be read, both for the reason that we read any other poetry, and because only by reading them can a stage production be aesthetically intelligible. Shakespeare wrote his plays to be performed – it is even possible, though most improbable, that it never occurred to him that they might be treated as literature to be read – and there is plenty of evidence to show how popular they were on the stage in his day; for example, Francis Meres writing in 1598: 'Shakespeare among the English is the most excellent in both kinds [i.e. tragedy and comedy] for the stage.' When Lamb wrote that 'the Lear of Shakespeare cannot be acted' he did not mean that Shakespeare was an incompetent dramatist, but that Kemble and Kean were incapable of acting the part, and this because, as Granville-Barker has shown, they attempted to act it with apparatus instead of with poetry. Yet it does not necessarily follow that the plays, the great tragedies in particular, are better when heard even in the theatre of Granville-Barker – would be better even in the Globe theatre itself with Shakespeare and Burbage on the stage (though one would give a fair slice of one's life to be there) – than when read in the study, and there are still those who, like Lamb, prefer their own reading of the poetry and their own imaginative interpretation to that imposed by the actors: 'It is difficult for a frequent playgoer to disembarrass the idea of Hamlet from the person and voice of Mr K. We speak of Lady Macbeth, while we are in reality thinking of Mrs Siddons.'[5] But whether we are stage-enthusiasts or not, we must, as the editors of the Folio wrote more than three hundred years ago, 'reade him, and againe, and againe', for it is the greatest poetry in the world, and for that reason so much the greatest drama.

The essential qualities of the artist, I take it, are three: an abnormally urgent instinct to create, an abnormally strong and sensitive imagination, and the skill to execute the demands of the creative impulse as dictated by the imagination. By imagination I mean the faculty that has a twofold power of transmutation, of translating something perceived (the stimulus, or impulse[6]), which may be superficially ugly,[7] into an experience or vision of beauty, and then of translating the experience into an equivalent of forms or sounds. For the primary product of the imaginative creation, the experience, cannot be directly communicated, it has to be transformed into a medium that can be sensuously apprehended, and which will, if the process is successful, communicate to the percipient something of the artist's visionary experience. The work of art is this substitute for the vision, the equivalent, or image, composed of new combinations of forms and colours if it is a sculpture or painting, of new combinations of sound if it is music or poetry. Shakespeare himself describes the twofold imaginative process:

INTRODUCTION

> And as imagination bodies forth
> The form of things unknown, the poet's pen
> Turns them into shapes, and gives to airy nothing
> A local habitation and a name.

In visual art the equivalent may, and very often does, resemble the stimulus, the thing that inspired the experience; on the other hand it may have little or even no resemblance.[8] The important point is that a work of art is always an equivalent, never a reproduction. In poetry there is, of course, no question of identity of stimulus and image, of the thing written about and the writing, but it is equally important to remember that the poetry does not lie in the thing described, however beautiful, in the thing said, however profound, but in the way of saying it: in the words, which intensify the primary and literal meaning and impose another of their own, logically inexpressible.

Poetry, then, is the image of this visionary experience, its equivalent expressed in words, with the additional qualification that the words are metrically related, for it is by the relationship (not only metrical or rhythmical) of the words, independently of, or only partly in conjunction with, their precise and logical meaning that the image is conveyed. The line, 'Nor did I wonder at the lily's white', is poetry not because of its rational meaning, its denotation, but because, as Coleridge would say, it is the best words in the best order. Poetry is made not with ideas but with words, and much of the delight of reading poetry is that of recognizing the object in the image, the thing described in the perfect equivalence of the words, in recognizing, that is, similarity in dissimilarity.

This verbal relationship may be onomatopoeic, which in its crudest form is as close as verbal imagery can approach to reproduction of the subject matter, the words themselves being an imitation of a sound or action, as in Ajax's unconsciously comic bombast in *Troilus and Cressida*:

> Thou, trumpet, there's my purse,
> Now crack thy lungs, and split thy brazen pipe:
> Blow villain, till thy sphered bias cheek
> Outswell the colic of puff'd Aquilon:
> Come, stretch thy chest, and let thy eyes spout blood.

Though this is not crude, for Shakespeare is rarely that, and there is much more than onomatopoeia in the lines, more subtly the words may suggest a quality instead of imitating the sense:

>   to reside
> In thrilling region of thick-ribbed ice.

Far more words are onomatopoeic in origin than is generally realized, their roots sunk deep in the remote times when prehistoric man began to evolve a language from sounds that were suggestive of the thing he wished to describe, or of the thought or emotion that he struggled to express, and certain words and combinations of words must have an elemental significance of which we are not consciously aware.[9] It is probable that, as there is a visual symbolism in dreams, there is in language an aural symbolism that is also part of the collective unconscious, so that if these symbols or primary images of words present themselves to the poet as perfect equivalents, in much the same way as do the secondary images of metaphor, they will evoke in the reader the imaginative experience that the poet is trying to communicate, and the recognition of that strange inevitability common to all great art. They will form the 'magic and evocatory phrase' of which Shakespeare is, above all other poets and at all stages of his career, the master:

INTRODUCTION

>   huge leviathans
> Forsake unsounded deeps to dance on sands.
> Triumph is become an ale-house guest.
> Like Arion on a dolphin's back.
> Venerable Nestor, hatch'd in silver.
> Darkling stand the varying shore o' the world.
>   human grace
> Affords them dust and shadow.

The conscious and more obvious form of onomatopoeia generally entails the employment of alliteration and assonance, as in Ajax's speech – *pipe, puff, split, spout; stretch, chest* – and it is as well to distinguish clearly between the two. Alliteration is the repetition of the same letter, generally at the beginning of, but also within, closely juxtaposed words; assonance is strictly the rhyming of words by means of the vowels only, as in Benedick's *lady – baby*. Assonance, therefore, is less concentrated and more widely distributed throughout a passage, less penetrating but more permeating; but as these vowel rhymes may be within the line and therefore close together, they become indistinguishable from vowel alliteration (for example, *thrilling* and *thick-ribbed*) so that for the sake of simplicity it is best to use alliteration to signify the close repetition of the same consonant, assonance the repetition of the same vowel, and by extension, of syllables of similar sound at more or less remote intervals, as in:

>   Safely in harbour
> Is the king's ship; in the deep nook, where once
> Thou call'dst me up at midnight to fetch dew
> From the still-vex'd Bermoothes, there she's hid:
> The mariners all under hatches stow'd;
> Who, with a charm join'd to their suffer'd labour,
> I have left asleep.

The Poetry of Shakespeare's Plays

The deep – asleep and *dew – who* are full rhymes, *fetch – vex, under – suffer, safely – labour, harbour – a charm* are assonantal, and though *harbour – labour* is half alliterative it is best regarded as assonance, the words being too far apart for any consonantal relationship to be effective without the support of their harmonized and harmonizing vowels. Assonance is the interplay of similar as well as of identical vowels, and in these lines from *The Tempest* is used, I suggest, with superlative effect.

Alliteration is most frequent in Shakespeare's early work, particularly in the explosive rhetoric of the histories, as when the captain in 2 *Henry VI* threatens Suffolk:

> By devilish policy art thou grown great,
> And, like ambitious Scylla, overgorged
> With gobbets of thy mother's bleeding hearts.

The device is beautifully employed by the disgraced Duchess of Gloucester in the same play:

> My shame will not be shifted with my sheet:
> No, it will hang upon my richest robes.

It is also common in the lyrical plays that followed the histories, in *Romeo and Juliet*, for example:

> How silver-sweet sound lovers' tongues by night,
> Like softest music to attending ears.

And alliteration, highly self-conscious, is an important element in the *Sonnets*, which Shakespeare was writing at the same time as the lyrical plays:

INTRODUCTION

And summer's green all girded up in sheaves,
Borne on the bier with white and bristly beard.

Since most of our words begin with a consonant, and the most forcible form of alliteration is initial, the young Shakespeare's fondness for the device is largely responsible for the importance of the consonants in his early poetry. In this early work alliteration is, on the whole, consciously emphatic and decorative, but in the later plays, particularly in *Macbeth*, it becomes an instrument of profound dramatic effect.

As alliteration is characteristic of the early poetry, so is assonance of the later; in the one the consonants are relatively more important, in the other the vowels, though a superficial comparison is apt to be misleading, as in the later poetry both figures are less obtrusive because less decorative and more structural. The earlier assonance is typically alliterative in effect because of its concentration, as in the opening speech of *Love's Labour's Lost*, in the first eight lines of which we have, *fame, brazen, grace, disgrace, bate, make, brave*:

Let fame, that all hunt after in their lives,
Live register'd upon our brazen tombs,
And then grace us in the disgrace of death...

Shakespeare's youthful fondness for wordplay makes this simple form of assonance more frequent and obvious; the antithesis *grace – disgrace*, for example, and such puns and quibbles as, 'Have not the grace to grace it with such show'.

Now compare the opening of *Love's Labour's Lost* with that of *Antony and Cleopatra*, written some fifteen years later:

The Poetry of Shakespeare's Plays

> Nay, but this dotage of our general's
> O'erflows the measure: those his goodly eyes,
> That o'er the files and musters of the war
> Have glow'd like plated Mars, now bend, now turn
> The office and devotion of their view
> Upon a tawny front: his captain's heart,
> Which in the scuffles of great fights hath burst
> The buckles on his breast, reneges all temper,
> And is become the bellows and the fan
> To cool a gipsy's lust. Look, where they come:
> Take but good note, and you shall see in him
> The triple pillar of the world transform'd
> Into a strumpet's fool.

Here, concentrated in the first five lines, is the group, *dotage, o'erflows, those, o'er, glow'd, devotion,* followed later by *bellows, note,* but less obvious, because more evenly distributed over the thirteen lines of the speech, is the sequence, *musters, front, scuffles, buckles, lust, strumpet's.* The effect of this counter-assonance, like the alliteration in *Macbeth,* is dramatic, the sequence of muted vowels forming an ominous undertone to the splendour suggested by the open *o*'s of the other group. It will be observed, too, that the assonantal words in the *Love's Labour's Lost* passage are mostly monosyllables, those in the *Antony and Cleopatra* disyllables, and this again is characteristic. But the full appreciation of Shakespeare's later assonance depends upon an appreciation of his rhythm, and this in turn involves a knowledge of his verse and its development.

The order in which Shakespeare wrote his plays is sufficiently established to make it possible to divide them into five fairly well-defined groups, though both classification and dates can be only approximate, and they give a somewhat misleading appearance of tidiness and certitude; *Julius Caesar*, for example, may have been written immediately after *Henry V*, and *Titus Andronicus* is grouped with the early comedies, *All's Well* and *Measure for Measure* with the tragedies.

EARLY HISTORIES AND COMEDIES 1590–94.
2 Henry VI, 3 Henry VI, Richard III, 1 Henry VI, The Comedy of Errors, Titus Adronicus, The Taming of the Shrew, The Two Gentlemen of Verona.

LYRICAL PLAYS 1594–97.
Love's Labour's Lost, Romeo and Juliet, Richard II, A Midsummer Night's Dream, King John, The Merchant of Venice.

HISTORICAL AND ROMANTIC COMEDIES 1597–1601.
1 Henry IV, 2 Henry IV, The Merry Wives of Windsor, Henry V, Much Ado about Nothing, As You Like It, Twelfth Night.

TRAGEDIES 1601–08.
Julius Caesar, Troilus and Cressida, Hamlet, All's Well that Ends Well, Measure for Measure, Othello, Macbeth, King Lear, Timon of Athens, Coriolanus, Antony and Cleopatra.

ROMANCES 1608–13.
Pericles, Cymbeline, The Winter's Tale, The Tempest, Henry VIII, The Two Noble Kinsmen.

The total number of lines in these thirty-eight plays (excluding the lines that are probably by another hand in *The Taming of the Shrew, Pericles, Henry VIII* and *The Two*

The Poetry of Shakespeare's Plays

Noble Kinsmen) is almost exactly 100,000, of which, in round figures, 28,000 are in prose, 7,000 in rhyme, and 65,000 in blank verse. The great preponderance of blank verse, two-thirds of the total, would in any event make some knowledge of its characteristics desirable, but the difference between the verse of Shakespeare's apprenticeship and of his complete mastery is so immense that it is essential; for there is no one Shakespearean style, no one Shakespearean poetry, but at least five, corresponding roughly to the periods given above. Something of this difference becomes immediately apparent on comparing extracts from two similar speeches written at an interval of twenty years, the first from Aegeon's narrative of his shipwreck in the *Comedy of Errors*, the second from Prospero's in *The Tempest*. The text is that of the Folio:

> At length another ship had seiz'd on vs,
> And knowing whom it was their hap to saue,
> Gaue healthfull welcome to their ship-wrackt guests,
> And would haue reft the Fishers of their prey,
> Had not their barke beene very slow of saile;
> And therefore homeward did they bend their course.
> Thus haue you heard me sever'd from my blisse,
> That by misfortunes was my life prolong'd,
> To tell sad stories of my owne mishaps.

> In few, they hurried vs a-boord a Barke,
> Bore vs some Leagues to Sea, where they prepared
> A rotten carkasse of a Butt, not rigg'd,
> Nor tackle, sayle, nor mast, the very rats
> Instinctiuely haue quit it: There they hoyst vs
> To cry to th' Sea, that roard to vs; to sigh

INTRODUCTION

   To th' windes, whose pitty sighing backe againe
   Did vs but louing wrong.

Not only do the passages sound very different, they even look different – because of the punctuation.

If the last two lines of the first passage and the last three and a half of the second are scanned in the orthodox way as a succession of stressed and unstressed syllables, the irregular feet will be distinguished; but it is unnatural to limit stress to two degrees of intensity, so that if we increase it to five, marking the most lightly stressed syllables 1, and the most heavily stressed 5 (2 4 representing the normal iambic foot), we get something like this:

| 2 3 | | 2 4 | | 2 3 | | 2 4 | | 2 4 \| |
| 2 4 | | 4 4 | | 2 2 | | 2 4 | | 2 4 \|\| |

2 4		2 3		2 4		2 || 4		2 4 3
2 5		2 1 5 |		2 5		2 3 ||		2 5
2 1 5 |		3 4		2 4		2 4		2 4
3 2		2 4		2 4 ||				

This distinguishes the absolutely irregular feet, the spondee (4 4) and the pyrrhic (2 2) in the first passage, in the second the redundant syllable at the end of the first line, the anapaests (2 1 5) and the trochee (3 2), but it also shows the irregularities within the iambic feet themselves, the lightly stressed second syllable of 2 3, and the very heavily stressed of 2 5. According to this analysis (and any such analysis must be subjective) the proportion of normal iambics to total feet in the first passage is 6 to 10, in the second 7 to 18, if we consider neither of the last two feet in the first line strictly regular, and it illustrates the way in which a secondary rhetorical, or speech, rhythm is mounted on the primary metrical one, so that when reading the verse we are aware of the two, the basic and regular iambic beat being interwoven with the varying rhythm, which sometimes coincides with but constantly eludes it, like the melodies in contrapuntal music.

But this is not all. The smallest unit in blank verse is the foot, the next is the line, and in *The Comedy of Errors* passage each line is regular, a complete grammatical unit defined by a stop. But in *The Tempest* extract none of the grammatical or rhetorical units coincides with the line; there are pauses after a first, second, third and fourth foot, and another in the middle of the fourth foot of the first line, but none at the end of the lines. Here, therefore, is an extension of the imposed rhythm: the mounting of the rhetorical unit on the basic unit of the line, so that again we are aware of a double movement, aware of the line structure even when it is overridden by the structural unit of the phrase or clause. Clearly, the rhythm of *The Tempest* is far more complex than that of *The Comedy of Errors*.

This imposition of one rhythm, the rhetorical, of which we are fully conscious, on another of which we are only half-consciously aware, is another form of the basic contrapuntal principle in art, the essential quality of poetry being, as argued above, the secondary meaning imposed on the literal sense by the words themselves, which secondary, but so much the most important, meaning is the equivalent of the poet's experience as transformed by his imagination. Both the words and rhythms of poetry – which are, of course, inseparable – are revelations of a profound harmony, of similarity in dissimilarity, and of an underlying unity in the apparent confusion of diversity. A third form of the same contrapuntal principle in poetry is that of the secondary imagery of metaphor, to be considered later.

INTRODUCTION

It is because of the contrapuntal rhythm of verse that it is better to confine the term 'poetry' to metrical writing. Prose has only one rhythm, a freer and, in the hands of a master, an infinitely varied rhythm it is true, which may be made to approximate to the double rhythm of verse by complex variations on one or more prosodic feet, but if it goes too far in the direction of regular repetition it crosses the ill-defined frontier between prose and verse. Then again, there is no artificial linear unit in prose, so that the imposition of variations on a basic norm of foot and line is denied to it, and with it the power to delight in the same degree as verse, by the alternating fulfilment and denial of anticipated repetition and by the resolution of competing rhythms. Things can be said in the artificial medium of verse that cannot possibly be said in prose: the lovemaking of Romeo and Juliet, for example.

It must be remembered that when Shakespeare began to write, blank verse was a new verse form in English. First used by the Earl of Surrey in the middle of the sixteenth century in his translation of the *Aeneid*, it was applied to the drama by Sackville and Norton in their tragedy of *Gorboduc* shortly before Shakespeare's birth, and developed in the eighties by his immediate predecessors, of whom Marlowe was the chief. Marlowe died in 1593, leaving to Shakespeare the task of bringing the undeveloped medium to full maturity. The typical Marlovian line is similar to those quoted from *The Comedy of Errors*: end-stopped, a slight pause in the sense after the second or third foot, sometimes sufficiently marked to require punctuation, and an occasional reversal of the first foot to form a trochee, as in *Edward II*:

Crŏwnĕts of pearl | about his naked arms,
And in his sportful hands | an olive tree.

The Poetry of Shakespeare's Plays

Such a medium is adequate for the expression of the rhetoric and pure poetry[10] of which Marlowe's plays are largely composed, but is much too inflexible, monotonous, artificial and limited to be adequate as a fully dramatic vehicle, for the expression of the full range of emotions. Though substantially the medium of the early rhetorical histories and lyrical comedies of Shakespeare, gradually at first, then more and more rapidly, he modified the restrictive metrical conventions, varying the line by frequent and diverse substitutions of feet, and varying the movement of the verse as a whole by running the lines into one another, and making the major or any minor pause after, or in the middle of, any foot. In this way Shakespeare transformed the plainsong, the monophonic verse of Marlowe into a new polyphonic or contrapuntal poetry of interwoven rhythms; as a writer of verse his progress is from angularity and regularity to plasticity and variety, as a writer of poetry, from artifice and diffuseness, by way of simplicity and restraint, to a dramatic naturalism and concentration, A few short extracts taken from plays written at intervals of about five years, and each falling, therefore, within one of the five periods given above, will illustrate the technical development.

The first comes from 2 *Henry VI* (*c.1590*), the words of Alexander Iden after killing Cade:

> Hence will I drag thee headlong by the heels
> Unto a dunghill which shall be thy grave,
> And there cut off thy most ungracious head;
> Which I will bear in triumph to the king,
> Leaving thy trunk for crows to feed upon.

The only irregularity is the reversal of the first foot in three of the lines. There are no mid-line pauses, but there is

INTRODUCTION

an example of the simplest form of overflow, the first line running over, not very forcibly, to the pause at the end of the second.

The further development of the run-on line may be illustrated from *Richard II* (*1595*), the main pause, or caesura, coming after the third foot, though the end of the sentence itself coincides with the end of a line:

> As if this flesh which walls about our life
> Were brass impregnable, and humour'd thus
> Comes at the last and with a little pin
> Bores through his castle wall, and farewell king!

In the five years between the writing of *Richard II* and *Twelfth Night* the transformation of blank verse had taken place, and rhetorical-lyrical had become dramatic poetry. Viola speaks:

> I see you what you are, you are too proud;
> But, if you were the devil, you are fair.
> My lord and master loves you: O, such love
> Could be but recompensed, though you were crown'd
> The nonpareil of beauty!

This illustrates two other forms of variety: the pause in the middle of a foot, after *devil* and *loves you*, and the ending of a speech in mid-line, here again in mid-foot. It was inevitable that after a comma within the line should come a period, and finally the end of the speech itself, and in *Twelfth Night* there is a big jump in the proportion of speeches that end in this way. Although there is no metrical irregularity, all the lines are different, owing simply to the shifting of the pause.

The Poetry of Shakespeare's Plays

A feminine ending is a redundant syllable at the end of a line, and this form of variety Shakespeare had always employed, but it becomes steadily more frequent as his style develops;[11] in the earliest plays about one line in seven has a feminine ending, in the latest the proportion is one in three. *Macbeth* (c.1605), from which the following extract is taken, has one in four:

> He hath a wisdom that doth guide his val|our
> To act in safe|ty. There is none but he
> Whose being I do fear: and under him
> My genius is rebuked, as it is said
> Mark Antony's was by Caes|ar. He chid the sis|ters...

The first and fifth lines have feminine endings, and in the second the pause in the middle of the third foot gives the same falling rhythm. But the fifth line is the interesting one, for the falling rhythm of *Caesar* really is equivalent to that of *sisters*, the last syllable being genuinely redundant, and defined by a period more strictly than that of *sisters* by the end of the overflowing line. These mid-line redundant syllables become increasingly common, and are a vital element in Shakespeare's rhythm, as will be shown later. They are, of course, scanned as the first syllable of an anapaest, but the effect of the break is that of the line ending, making them into a redundant syllable followed by an iambus. There is a genuine anapaest in this fifth line as well, bringing the total number of syllables to thirteen:

> Mārk Ān|tŏnў's wās | bў Cāes|ăr. ‖ Hĕ chĭd | thĕ sīs|tĕrs...

Five or six years later came *The Tempest* and the full perfection of the medium which now, with its complex contrapuntal rhythm and assonance, approaches music on

INTRODUCTION

the one hand, and on the other the medium of the sculptor and potter, so plastic is it that the verse gives the impression of having been modelled out of a homogeneous material, not constructed after selection from a multitude of words. The speech is Alonso's in III, iii:

> O, it is monstrous, monstrous!
> Methought the billows spoke, and told me of it;
> The wind did sing it to me; and the thunder,
> That deep and dreadful organ-pipe, pronounced
> The name of Prosper: it did bass my trespass.
> Therefore my son i' th' ooze is bedded; and
> I'll seek him deeper than e'er plummet sounded,
> And with him there lie mudded.

Mid-line pauses in the earlier verse are generally after the second or third foot, and these are always the most common; then come pauses within the three middle feet, after the first and fourth, and in the middle of the first and fifth, as in the lines taken from the same scene:

> Which here, in this most desolate isle, else falls...
> Who, though they are of monstrous shape, yet, note...

In the sixth line of Alonso's speech the pause is in the middle of the fifth foot, characteristically after a disyllable (*bedded*), and is followed by the final weekly stressed *and*. There are some parts of speech that are so closely attached to the next word that there is often no question of a pause between the two, in particular, conjunctions and prepositions, so that a line ending with one of these weakly stressed proclitic words makes an extreme form of enjambment, or run-on line, 'and/I'll seek him' being a good example. These were called 'weak' endings by J K Ingram, who distinguished them from the 'light' endings of final pronouns and auxiliaries, which are a shade more heavily stressed.[12] Weak endings are rare; there are only twenty in all the plays before *Coriolanus* and *Antony and Cleopatra*, which have forty-four and twenty-eight respectively. There are more light endings, an average of about five in the plays before *Antony and Cleopatra*, which again leaps to seventy-one.

If now we begin to scan the speech, the first half-line runs:

Ō, ĭt | ĭs mōn|strŏus, mōn|strŏus!

And it does seem monstrous to force the lines into an iambic pattern that cuts right across the natural rhythm:

O, it is | mónstrous, | mónstrous!

Not only are the syllables in the iambic feet split by pauses, but the repeated disyllabic *monstrous* is itself unnaturally dismembered. And consider the penultimate line. This must be spoken with a falling trochaic rhythm, partly because of the feminine ending, but mainly because three of the words are natural trochees:

I'll séek him | déeper | than e'er | plúmmet | sóunded.

This illustrates another way in which Shakespeare, particularly in his later plays, imposes a secondary rhythm on the primary iambics.

In this late poetry Shakespeare carries foot substitution to its extreme limit, as in the line:

Fātĕd | tŏ thĕ | pūrpŏse | dĭd Ăntōn|ĭŏ ōp|ĕn,

where all the feet are irregular. The limit, of course, is the critical point at which the iambic pattern begins to disintegrate, which roughly speaking is when, over a series of lines, the iambics are outnumbered by alien feet. Yet the wonder is that this verse never loses its essential iambic structure in spite of the constant reversal of the rhythm. This is because the trochaic movement is in the main a false one, not a real reversal of the foot, but a suggested reversal. There is a genuine trochee and real reversal in the first foot of 'Thérefore, my son i' th' ooze is bedded', and the famous line of Lear is a complete reversal, 'Never, never, never, never, never'; but there is no real reversal in the lines, 'To act in safety. There is none but he', 'Mark Antony's was by Caesar. He chid the sisters', the trochaic movement being merely a suggested one: *safety*, by the pause in the middle of the foot, *sisters*, because the last syllable of the word is the last of the line and metrically redundant, *Caesar*, because the last syllable comes before a mid-line period, and like a feminine ending is redundant. All three words are disyllables, which emphasizes the trochaic effect, as can be seen by comparing the monosyllabic feminine ending of 'Methought the billows spoke, and told me of it'.

Now consider Alonso's speech. It will readily be admitted that these constitute the majority of the important words: *monstrous, monstrous, billows, thunder, dreadful, organ, Prosper, trespass, bedded, deeper, plummet, sounded, mudded.* All are natural trochees, and such a concentration would in itself be sufficient to suggest a trochaic rhythm, although there are only two trochaic feet in the passage; but when four of the words form feminine endings and three make mid-foot pauses the counter-rhythm becomes irresistible. Then the effect is intensified by juxtaposition – *monstrous monstrous, dreadful organ, plummet sounded* – and again greatly intensified – and this is the point I particularly wish to make – by the assonantal relationship of the words. *Prosper* is the central word, both in significance and position, and to it are linked both by rhythm and assonance, *monstrous, trespass, deeper, thunder*, which links *Prosper* to the sequence *plummet, mudded,* modulating into *bedded, sounded*. There is no need to insist on the exact assonantal relationship of the words, but that the majority are associated is clear enough.

This combination of rhythm and assonance, each emphasizing the other, adds another quality to the later poetry, in which whole speeches are integrated and harmonized by the complex contrapuntal interweaving of a double rhythm with a melodic theme. Its development can be traced in the earlier work, but this, as has already been observed, is remarkable chiefly for its more concentrated alliteration and assonance, and not for the assonantal and trochaic sequence; inevitably so, for these sequences depend for their full effect on the developed and perfected rhythm. Beautiful as is the early poetry of Shakespeare, it has been rivalled by others, by Spenser and Marlowe, but the varied splendour of his later poetry has never been approached. There is nothing quite comparable, even in the harmonies of Milton, whose rhythm is far more formal, partly because it is not associated with the feminine ending, of which he makes little use, though sometimes he magnificently exploits natural trochees in conjunction with the mid-foot pause:

> All in a moment through the gloom were seen
> Ten thousand banners rise into the air
> With orient colours waving: with them rose
> A forest huge of spears; and thronging helms
> Appear'd, and serried shields in thick array
> Of depth immeasurable. Anon they move

INTRODUCTION

In perfect phalanx to the Dorian mood
Of flutes and soft recorders; such as rais'd
To height of noblest temper heroes old
Arming to battle.

But I open at random my copy of *Antony and Cleopatra*, and read:

I am dying, Egypt, dying; only
I here importune death awhile, until
Of many thousand kisses the poor last
I lay upon thy lips.

The first line, like Lear's fivefold 'never', is composed entirely of trochees, forming a complete and genuine reversal of the rhythm, a movement that is extended in the apparent reversal of 'many thousand kisses' and its harmonically related natural trochees. And finally consider the lines of Caeser, in which the eddying movement of the reed is suggested by the imposition of a complex rhythm of false trochees and dactyls:

And the ebb'd man, ne'er loved till ne'er worth love,
Comes dear'd by being lack'd. This common body,
Like to a vagabond flag upon the stream,
Goes to and back, lackeying the varying tide,
To rot itself with motion.

So far, two of the main elements in Shakespeare's poetry have been considered: the words, which are the image or equivalent of the poet's aesthetic experience, and the rhythmical relationship of the words. Both are contrapuntal, the significance of the words themselves in their complex pattern of sound and connotation being mounted on the literal meaning, which is itself greatly intensified in the process, and the free rhetorical rhythm being mounted on the tied metrical one. These, indeed, are the only essential elements in poetry:

Music to hear, why hear'st thou music sadly?

Be not afeard; the isle is full of noises
Sounds and sweet airs, that give delight and hurt not.

But in Caesar's speech there is another element: the comparison of the eddying reed to a sycophantic follower.

It is true that simile and metaphor are things inessential to poetry, but it is equally true that spontaneous and illuminating imagery is one of the most potent forces in poetry. Aristotle even goes so far as to say, 'The greatest thing of all by far is to be a master of metaphor. It is the one thing that cannot be learned from others: and it is also a sign of original genius, since a good metaphor implies the intuitive perception of the similarity in dissimilars.' Here then is a third form of the contrapuntal, or at least harmonic, principle in poetry. As the words are an image of the experience, and the imposed rhythm a reflection of the emotion and an echo of the basic metre, so metaphor is an image of the thing described; and as the reader recognizes with a shock of delight the equivalence of the experience and the words, of the emotion and the rhythm, so does he recognize the equivalence, the essential harmony, of the thing described and the secondary image of the metaphor. For we take a natural delight in this recognition of a real unity in apparent diversity, and the revelation of this fundamental harmony is the preoccupation of the artist.

Shakespeare is above all other poets the master of this secondary form of imagery; 'Every word in him is a picture', wrote the poet Gray, and though this is an exaggeration, it is true that almost every line contains an image, often more than one, and that this imagery is an element that goes to make his poetry so much the greatest in our language. But he was not always a master of what may be called the dramatic image, the image that is inseparable from character and action, any more than he was always a master of dramatic poetry; the development of his imagery runs parallel to that of his style as a whole, for only by a modification of the imagery could the style become fully dramatic.

Shakespeare was a lyric poet before he was a dramatic poet, and it was only natural that when he took to the writing of plays he should apply to them the kind of ornament with which he was familiar in the works of Spenser and the other Elizabethans, a conventional and ready-made imagery that was in the main symbolic and literary, derived from precious stones and materials, from sun and moon, from flowers and animals and classical mythology, in which tears are pearls, lips coral, cheeks roses, the lily and Diana the emblems of chastity, Hebe of youthful beauty, and the canker-worm of corruption. It is in the early poems, *Venus and Adonis* and *Lucrece*, that he employs this artificial imagery most extravagantly, and in Sonnet 21 he deprecates the practice of:

Making a couplement of proud compare
With sun and moon, with earth and sea's rich gems,
With April's first-born flowers and all things rare,

and in Sonnet 130 he satirizes it:

My mistress' eyes are nothing like the sun;
Coral is far more red than her lips' red:
If snow be white, why then her breasts are dun;

The Poetry of Shakespeare's Plays

> If hair be wires, black wires grow on her head.
> I have seen roses damask'd, red and white,
> But no such roses see I in her cheeks...

Yet there is much of this couplement of proud compare in the early plays, though not so elaborately developed, as when in *The Two Gentlemen of Verona* Proteus describes the sorrows of Silvia:

> A sea of melting pearl, which some call tears,
> Those at her father's churlish feet she tender'd;
> With them, upon her knees, her humble self,
> Wringing her hands, whose whiteness so became them
> As if but now they waxed pale for woe.

This is what may be called the lyrical form of this emblematic and literary imagery: the application to the plays of the stock ornament of pure poetry. It is clearly less appropriate for the rhetorical and anything but lyrical early histories, and here it takes another form, derived in part from the unnatural history and science of Lyly's *Euphues*, in which the snake is the symbol of perfidy, the kite of rapacity, the crocodile of hypocrisy, fire of love, and so on, and these plays are full of images such as this from 2 *Henry VI*:

> Beguiles him, as the mournful crocodile
> With sorrow snares relenting passengers,
> Or as the snake roll'd in the flowering bank,
> With shining checker'd slough, doth sting a child.

There is, of course, lyrical emblematic imagery in the histories as well, and all the comedies have the rhetorical Euphuistic variety, parodied by Falstaff in 1 *Henry IV*: 'For

INTRODUCTION

though the camomile, the more it is trodden on the faster it grows, yet youth, the more it is wasted the sooner it wears.'

But it is not only that much of the imagery of the early plays is derivative, unoriginal and unobserved; it is often developed at such length as to become a lyrical or rhetorical episode with claims to be considered as a decorative unit in its own right, independent almost of the play, as in Montague's description of the love-sick Romeo:

> Many a morning hath he there been seen,
> With tears augmenting the fresh morning's dew,
> Adding to clouds more clouds with his deep sighs:
> But all so soon as the all-cheering sun
> Should in the farthest east begin to draw
> The shady curtains from Aurora's bed,
> Away from light steals home my heavy son...

Beautiful as this is, in the Spenserean manner, it is quite clearly undramatic; all consideration of the advancement of the action and of the development of character is suspended while the simple image is deliberately unfolded and displayed to the audience with all manner of elaborations. It is the method of the *Sonnets*, which Shakespeare was then writing, but it is not the method of *Macbeth* and *King Lear*, or even of *As You Like It* and *Twelfth Night*.

The difference between Shakespeare's early imagery and his later is, then, partly one of originality, partly one of speed, though in the lyrical plays we often find an image that is basically conventional quite transfigured by his imagination and charged with an entirely new emotive energy, as when Romeo employs the stock comparisons of honey – sweetness, red and white:

35

The Poetry of Shakespeare's Plays

> Death, that hath suck'd the honey of thy breath,
> Hath had no power yet upon thy beauty:
> Thou art not conquer'd; beauty's ensign yet
> Is crimson in thy lips and in thy cheeks,
> And death's pale flag is not advanced there.

Shakespeare never wrote more beautifully than this, and here, in Romeo's last speech, he can afford to take his time, developing one fanciful image after another, though significantly he closes with a concentrated figure that combines the formal image of lips as the doors of breath with the original and arresting one of death as an unscrupulously acquisitive merchant: 'significantly', because the mixing, or apparent mixing of metaphors is characteristic of a later style.

Another cause, perhaps the fundamental one, of the slow and erratic movement of the early poetry is the exuberant delight that Shakespeare as a young man and an artist took in the potentialities of his medium, exploiting words to the extreme limit of their capacities, and even beyond, fretting and stretching them with almost childlike glee into curious contortions and fantastic combinations, sometimes working them unmercifully until they collapsed from exhaustion to lie as so much lifeless matter in his verse. There is a simple example of this wordplay in Montague's speech, in the pun *all-cheering sun – heavy son*, and in the punning antithesis, *light-heavy*, which Shakespeare was never able to resist. But this is cold modesty in comparison with the perverse ingenuity of Constance and Pandulph in *King John*:

> O, if thou grant my need,
> Which only lives but by the death of faith,
> That need must needs infer this principle,
> That faith would live again by death of need.

INTRODUCTION

> O then, tread down my need, and faith mounts up;
> Keep my need up, and faith is trodden down!

A pun may be no more than a superficial and tiresome play upon words, but it may be an elementary form of imagery, the imaginative fusion of two meanings of a word or phrase, and a good pun may have the illuminating and affective quality of metaphor, as when Romeo drinks the poison to the toast, 'Here's to my love!', and Hamlet forces the poisoned wine down Claudius' throat to the ferocious question, 'Is thy union here?' But the early puns of Shakespeare rarely have such dramatic significance; they are for the most part jingles – 'For Suffolk's duke, may he be suffocate' – or if imaginatively conceived as metaphor, self-consciously and deliberately developed into quibbling wordplay in the manner of Constance. And as the pun, a perception of similarity of sound in dissimilarity of sense, may be expanded into a quibble, so the metaphor, analogous to the pun, but a perception of similarity of quality in things otherwise unlike, may be expanded into a conceit, either by elaborating the common quality, or by trying to force other qualities into correspondence. Thus, when Arthur in *King John* pleads with Hubert for his eyes, he says that the hot iron will quench itself and rust away by drinking his tears, that it has strewn ashes on its head and died of grief, and that if revived it will glow with shame, and, like a dog, snap at its master.

Both quibble and conceit are diffuse and undramatic devices that are partly responsible for the leisurely pace of Shakespeare's early verse, but they, or at least the conceits when not too far-fetched, like the lyrical and rhetorical episodes of which they may form a part, are often extremely beautiful. They are of the essence of the poetry, but they may have little or nothing to do with the play. After the plays of the lyrical period they are much rarer, though Shakespeare always retained an affection for the pun, using it with consummate effect in the tragedies at times of the highest tension, sometimes in the form of dramatic irony, as when the mad Lear says to the blind Gloucester, 'Your eyes are in a heavy case, your purse in a light'.

Another form of imagery characteristic of the early and lyrical plays is personification. Of course, personification is often implicit in metaphor, and in this form is common throughout the works, most striking indeed in the last play of the canon, *Henry VIII*, where such images as this are frequent:

> who set the body and the limbs
> Of this great sport together?

And one of the favourite metaphors of the tragedies and romances is that of 'the sides of the earth'. A simpler form of implied personification is also common, as when the king in *All's Well* speaks of 'The inaudible and noiseless foot of Time', but direct personification like that in *Troilus and Cressida*, of Time with a wallet at his back, becomes less frequent. This early form of personification is akin to that in the morality plays, which were still being acted in Shakespeare's youth, and to that in Spenser's allegorical *Faerie Queene*, in both of which the characters are abstractions. Thus in *The Rape of Lucrece*, Lucrece rails at great length at Night, Opportunity and Time, and in *King John* the Bastard addresses thirty lines to 'That smooth-faced gentleman, tickling Commodity'. *King John* is remarkable for the amount of its direct personification, sometimes developed into a conceit, as when Constance so pitifully imagines Grief to have taken the place of her lost son:

INTRODUCTION

> Grief fills the room up of my absent child,
> Lies in his bed, walks up and down with me,
> Puts on his pretty looks, repeats his words...

and calls on Death to claim her as his wife, the strained passion and imagery of which is far removed from the simple, compact and highly dramatic image of Hamlet, 'this fell sergeant, death, Is strict in his arrest'.

It is not true, of course, that all the images in the early plays are conventional and highly developed ornamental details detachable from the whole, but simply that such images in an extreme form are characteristic, almost peculiar to them; and as there are plenty of examples of a modified artificial imagery in the later plays, particularly in the latest of all, so there is a host of brief and original, vivid and observed images in the earlier ones. Nor can it be said that the typical later images are better than the earlier, those in *Antony and Cleopatra* and *The Tempest* better than those in *Romio and Juliet* and *A Midsummer Night's Dream*; they are more dramatic, but that they are greater poetry is another matter. It can be said, however, that there is a remarkable change in the imagery after the plays of the lyrical period.

The last play of the lyrical series is *The Merchant of Venice*, and it is interesting to compare its opening with that of *1 Henry IV*, the first of the series of historical comedies:

> Your mind is tossing on the ocean;
> There, where your argosies with portly sail.
> Like signiors and rich burghers on the flood,
> Or, as it were, the pageants of the sea,
> Do overpeer the petty traffickers
> That curtsy to them, do them reverence,
> As they fly by them with their woven wings.

> So shaken as we are, so wan with care,
> Find we a time for frighted peace to pant,
> And breathe short-winded accents of new broils
> To be commenced in stronds afar remote.
> No more the thirsty entrance of this soil
> Shall daub her lips with her own children's blood...
> The edge of war, like an ill-sheathed knife,
> No more shall cut his master.

The words of Mercury are harsh after the songs of Apollo, or at least the words of Henry of England are more of this world than is the ethereal music of Venice and Belmont. Peace and England are personified, but briefly and with only a trace of the earlier conceit, and in a simple simile war is compared to a knife. These short similes are particularly characteristic: 'like a comet', 'like a robe pontifical'; *As You Like It* is full of them, though many are in prose, and it is significant that in 1 *Henry IV* Falstaff and the Prince invent seven similes for melancholy. Most of these images are original and arresting, and follow one another in an orderly sequence, so that though the pace of the verse as a whole is retarded by them it moves steadily without the delays occasioned by a fully developed conceit or lyrical episode. The imagery, like the style in general, is chastened, though there are exceptions, as when in 1 *Henry IV* Vernon describes the Prince of Wales and his comrades, in 2 *Henry IV* the king apostrophizes Sleep, in *Henry V* the Archbishop of Canterbury, remembering his *Euphues*, compares the commonwealth of man to that of the bees, in *As You Like It* Jaques compares the world to a stage, and in *Twelfth Night* Orsino moralizes on music.

The action is no longer subordinated to the imagery, but imagery is subdued to the action, and metaphor, stripped of its elaborations, assumes a new form. In the early poetry, in

INTRODUCTION

which the line is so emphatically the unit, a favourite form of short metaphor is that of a noun followed by a prepositional phrase:

The coward conquest of a wretch's knife.
The barren tender of a poet's debt.
And shake the yoke of inauspicious stars.

There are examples of this type of line in 1 *Henry IV*, though not many:

The moody frontier of a servant brow.

Much more common is the metaphor in the form of paired verbs[13] or adjectives:

Why, look you, I am whipp'd and scourged with rods,
Nettled and stung with pismires.

And he hath brought us smooth and gentle news.

Why, what a wasp-stung and impatient fool.

And then there is the metaphor contained in paired nouns:

Who is sweet Fortune's minion and her pride.

This is a variation of the old form, in which it might occur as 'the tresur'd minion of sweet Fortune', but Shakespeare preferred to combine the old and sonorous form of noun – prepositional phrase with the new device of paired words, and by a simple reversal created the type of metaphor that becomes almost a hallmark of his middle style. In this new idiom, 'sweet Fortune's minion and her pride' would read 'the pride and minion of sweet Fortune', and thus we have in 1 *Henry IV*:

> For the hot vengeance and the rod of heaven.
> The very bottom and the soul of hope.
> The quality and hair of our attempt.

As we should expect, there are a few similar constructions in the earlier plays; there are two brilliant ones in *The Merchant of Venice*, and there is even an example in *The Comedy of Errors*:

> What is the course and drift of your compact?

But this last resembles the others in construction only, *course* and *drift* being almost synonyms, whereas in all the others one of the paired nouns gives the general or literal sense, the other the particular or metaphorical; typically, one is monosyllabic, concrete and Saxon, the other polysyllabic, abstract and Latin in origin, as *rod – vengeance, hair – quality*. The same is true, with qualifications, of the paired adjectives and verbs, and it is this double impact of the abstract and general reinforced by the concrete and particular that makes this type of metaphor so arresting and illuminating; in Shakespeare's mind the appropriate image is at once suggested by the idea, and the one is imposed on the other.[14]

This form of metaphor first becomes conspicuous by its frequency in *Troilus and Cressida* – 'Swing and rudeness of his poise', 'sinew and the forehand of our host' – an indication that it was written, or possibly rewritten, shortly before *Hamlet*, in which it reaches its climax. Thus in the first act we have: gross and scope of my opinion, covenant and carriage of the article designed, dead vast and middle of the night, perfume and suppliance of a minute, voice and

INTRODUCTION

yielding of that body, shot and danger of desire, morn and liquid dew of youth, pith and marrow of our attribute, pales and forts of reason; and in addition there are several similar constructions: a fashion and a toy in blood, high and palmy state of Rome, and so on. But apart from this characteristic form, much of the imagery of *Hamlet* is very different from anything that had gone before; in place of the single elaborated image of the lyrical plays, of the steady sequence of clear-cut and almost businesslike images of the middle comedies and histories, there is a process of crystallization, fission and dissolution of images, so rapid that it is impossible to distinguish each one separately before its place is usurped by another. Consider Hamlet's speech to his mother:

> Such an act
> That blurs the grace and blush of modesty,
> Calls virtue hypocrite, takes off the rose
> From the fair forehead of an innocent love,
> And sets a blister there; makes marriage vows
> As false as dicers' oaths. O, such a deed
> As from the body of contraction plucks
> The very soul, and sweet religion makes
> A rhapsody of words.

The typical image of the lyrical plays is concentric, expanding like a bubble about its centre; the imagery of the next period is linear, a progress of well-defined and lively figures which, however, do not compete unduly for attention; but Hamlet's imagery is centrifugal, flying off from the centre like sparks from a Catherine wheel, splitting and creating new images in the process. Of this extraordinary reproduction of images by fission Hazlitt writes:

The Poetry of Shakespeare's Plays

> His [Shakespeare's] language abounds in sudden transitions and elliptical expressions. This is the source of his mixed metaphors, which are only abbreviated forms of speech. These, however, give no pain from long custom. They have, in fact, become idioms in the language. They are the building, and not the scaffolding to thought. We take the meaning and effect of a well-known passage entire, and no more stop to scan and spell out the particular words and phrases, than the syllables of which they are composed.

And this, as Mr Middleton Murry has observed, is because 'we have not, and are not intended to have, time to unfold his metaphors... His success, when we examine it, is not really so surprising, for the extent to which images are discordant depends upon the extent to which we unfold them, and that is wholly within the great poet's control, for it in turn depends primarily upon the rhythm and tempo of his writing.' The imagery of the early plays is much of it undramatic because we have time to unfold, and are expected to examine, the elaborated figures; the pace of the verse is unrelated to that of the action. But in *Hamlet*, and with increasing consistency in the plays that follow, the imagery is dramatic because it is generated by the action, and we have neither time, nor are we expected, to examine each fleeting and embryonic figure.

But the imagery of *Hamlet* as a whole has not the concentration and intensity of the passage quoted above; indeed, in his next speech Hamlet describes his dead father in the earlier conventional idiom:

Hyperion's curls, the front of Jove himself,
An eye like Mars, to threaten and command;

INTRODUCTION

> A station like the herald Mercury
> New-lighted on a heaven-kissing hill.

Then, after all, the new form of metaphor, 'the grace and blush of modesty', derives from the sonorous end-stopped line of the *Sonnets*, and is something at odds with the developing secondary rhythm that overflows the line; and not only rhythmically, but dramatically as well, it is a rather cumbersome unit in the verse now that every line is needed to support the massive content of the tragedies. 'Heaven's face' is briefer than 'the face of heaven', certainly briefer than 'the face and feature of the heavens', and the paired nouns of the metaphor become rarer after *Hamlet*,[15] the image being more frequently employed in its simplest form of a single word.

Macbeth was written probably four or five years after *Hamlet*, and illustrates this tauter and more concentrated imagery. Almost the only example of the paired-noun image is Macbeth's 'bank and shoal of time', and the double image is often contained in epithet and noun: 'ruin's wasteful entrance', 'night's yawning peal', 'life's fitful fever'. Old and expansive forms are compressed, as in Lady Macbeth's fourfold image:

> memory, the warder of the brain,
> Shall be a fume, and the receipt of reason
> A limbec only.

And she gives new life to the conceit by couching it in the form of a series of rhetorical questions, the detail of which is no more expected to be examined than are the questions to be answered:

The Poetry of Shakespeare's Plays

> Was the hope drunk
> Wherein you dress'd yourself? hath it slept since?
> And wakes it now, to look so green and pale
> At what it did so freely?

The image, as here, is packed into a single word: pity rides, ambition vaults, business is masked, grief whispers, night strangles, life is a fever, death dusty, a shadow, an actor, an idiot's tale. The difference between the imagery of the lyrical period and that of the tragedies is well illustrated by comparing Macbeth's simple, 'my way of life Is fall'n into the sear, the yellow leaf', with the opening of Sonnet 73, which might equally well come from *Romeo and Juliet*:

> That time of year thou mayst in me behold
> When yellow leaves, or none, or few, do hang
> Upon those boughs which shake against the cold,
> Bare ruin'd choirs, where late the sweet birds sang.

Similarly, the difference between the imagery of *Hamlet* in those parts where the action slackens, and that of *Antony and Cleopatra* may be illustrated by a comparison of Ophelia's speech on Hamlet with Cleopatra's on Antony, quoted on page 209:

> The expectancy and rose of the fair state,
> The glass of fashion and the mould of form,
> The observ'd of all observers, quite, quite down!
> And I, of ladies most deject and wretched,
> That suck'd the honey of his music vows,
> Now see that noble and most sovereign reason,
> Like sweet bells jangled, out of tune and harsh;
> That unmatch'd form and feature of blown youth
> Blasted with ecstasy.

INTRODUCTION

The difference is primarily one of style as a whole, and admirably demonstrates what was said above, that the paired-noun image is at odds with the developing rhythm. In Ophelia's speech the first and last lines are completely taken up with this form of image, the second is a variation of it, as are the paired adjectives of the other lines, and the whole is made up of a series of self-contained lines of similar structure. Though the imagery itself is brilliantly kaleidoscopic – particularly the confusion of taste and sound in the variation of the conventional 'honey breath' theme: 'That suck'd the honey of his music vows' – the pace is that of the singly developed image of the earlier style. Cleopatra's speech is much less formal in construction, moving to a far more liberal rhythm, and a progressive and elemental imagery of ocean, air and earth.

After the passion that expressed itself in the great tragedies in imagery derived from disease and sickness, tormented bodies and beasts of prey, Shakespeare seems to have turned with relief to themes that invited the more lyrical utterance of his early years. *Antony and Cleopatra*, like *Romeo and Juliet*, evokes the emotion of pity, but not, like its immediate predecessors, that of terror as well; it is the link between the tragedies and romances, and contains hints of Shakespeare's return in the latest plays to the pure poetry and artificial imagery of his youth. Thus, the obscure schoolmaster, Euphronius, is immortalized by his lyrical presentation of his credentials:

> Such as I am I come from Antony:
> I was of late as petty to his ends
> As is the morn-dew on the myrtle-leaf
> To his grand sea.

THE POETRY OF SHAKESPEARE'S PLAYS

And Charmian, with a wonderful mingling of the simple, trivial and conventional, addresses the dead Cleopatra:

> Now boast thee, death, in thy possession lies
> A lass unparallel'd. Downy windows, close;
> And golden Phoebus never be beheld
> Of eyes again so royal! Your crown's awry;
> I'll mend it, and then play.

This conventional and periphrastic imagery is a minor characteristic of the romances, though its effect is strangely different from that in the early plays. There its formality is matched by the verse, but here it is in sharp contrast to the almost negligent ease of the rhythm and the simple diction and natural allusions by which it is so often accompanied:

>   violets dim,
> But sweeter than the lids of Juno's eyes
> Or Cytherea's breath; pale primroses,
> That die unmarried, are they can behold
> Bright Phoebus in his strength...

This combination of art and nature adds a peculiar charm to the late poetry.

Shakespeare was interested in all the arts, and probably practised some of them other than poetry. Almost certainly he was a musician, and that he was something of a painter is suggested by his collaboration with Burbage at the beginning of 1613 in the designing of Lord Rutland's *impresa*, a painted paper shield displayed at a tilt in the manner described in *Pericles*, II. ii. Either he was acquainted with and admired the paintings of Pieter Brueghel the elder, or he had a similar eye for humorous and realistic detail, for all through his works there are vignettes that recall pictures by that Flemish master.

In *Lucrece*:

> Here one man's hand lean'd on another's head,
> His nose being shadow'd by his neighbour's ear;
> Here one being throng'd bears back, all boll'n and red;
> Another smother'd seems to pelt and swear.

In *King John*:

> I saw a smith stand with his hammer, thus,
> The whilst his iron did on the anvil cool,
> With open mouth swallowing a tailor's news;
> Who, with his shears and measure in his hand,
> Standing on slippers, which his nimble haste
> Had falsely thrust upon contrary feet...

In 1 *Henry IV*:

>   fickle changelings and poor discontents,
> Which gape and rub the elbow at the news
> Of hurly-burly innovation.

In *Coriolanus*:

>   woollen vassals, things created
> To buy and sell with groats, to show bare heads
> In congregations, to yawn, be still and wonder...

Iachimo is an amateur of the arts, describing with gusto the Renaissance detail of Imogen's bedchamber, and maintaining that 'the shrine of Venus, or straight-pight Minerva' are 'postures beyond brief nature'; and it is significant that the device of Hermione's statue, 'newly performed' by 'that rare Italian master, Julio Romano', is Shakespeare's addition to the original story.

Most of Shakespeare's imagery is taken from nature, but much is taken from the arts, from all the arts. Palaces and monuments and pyramids are common images throughout the plays, from Romeo's 'palace of dim night' to Prospero's cloud-capped towers and gorgeous palaces, and building and architectural images are particularly frequent in *Henry IV*. In addition to painting and sculpture, dancing, weaving, metal-work, carpentry and the other applied arts are drawn upon, and music in all its forms, vocal and instrumental, and the instruments themselves are among the commonest of the images.

The imagery, however, is a reflection not only of the sights and sounds of nature and art, but of all manner of other impressions, for all Shakespeare's faculties were most delicately attuned and receptive, and his sense of taste, smell and touch has each its contribution to make to the poetry. Thus, in the first speech in *Twelfth Night*, Orsino compares music to food, and a particularly beautiful cadence to the scent of violets, and as examples of tactile images we may take Henry IV's representation of his own disposition as 'smooth as oil, soft as young down', and Othello's description of Desdemona's skin as 'smooth as monumental alabaster'. Shakespeare, we may be sure, is speaking in the person of Biron when, in *Love's Labour's Lost,* he eulogizes the physical senses, quickened by love:

> A lover's eyes will gaze an eagle blind;
> A lover's ear will hear the lowest sound...
> Love's feeling is more soft and sensible
> Than are the tender horns of cockled snails;
> Love's tongue proves dainty Bacchus gross in taste.

Visual images, however, are much the most frequent, for it is above all the eyes that are the most precious of man's possessions, beautiful in themselves, and themselves the main source of beauty in this delightful world; and 'precious' is the epithet applied by Shakespeare to the eyes throughout his work, from Rosaline's 'dear and precious eyesight' and Romeo's 'precious treasure of his eyesight', to Othello's 'darling like your precious eye' and Edgar's tragic punning image of the blind Gloucester 'with his bleeding rings, Their precious stones new lost'.

One other aspect of the imagery remains to be considered: its unifying and harmonizing quality. If all this host of images in a play were independent and unrelated flashes illuminating the multifarious detail, the effect might be bewildering, a distraction, and this fitful illumination a disintegrating force. But they are not independent and unrelated; for one thing, running throughout all the plays there is a broad underlying pattern of images taken from nature and from what Dr Spurgeon calls 'domestic' subjects, reflections of Shakespeare's everyday experiences and impressions, images such as Lady Macbeth's 'blanket of the dark', and Macbeth's equally homely and tragic, 'What rhubarb, senna, or what purgative drug, Would scour these English hence?' Then again, there is a pattern common to the plays of a certain group; for example, in the histories, more particularly in the early histories, the recurrent image of the sun as the emblem of kingship, of beasts and birds of prey as types of the treacherous and rapacious leaders of York and Lancaster, of a tree planted, dismembered, and hacked down or rooted up, as a symbol of the making and unmaking of kings and great houses; thus, in 3 *Henry VI* the kingmaker Warwick punningly boasts, 'I'll plant Pantagenet, root him up who dares', then when he changes sides promises 'to replant Henry in his former state', and dies with the words, 'Thus yields the cedar to the axe's edge'.

This is a fairly obvious and conscious symbolism, but it is improbable that Shakespeare was conscious of the much more subtle symbolism of the imagery that is peculiar to a single play. It is as though he was so possessed by the theme of each of his great tragedies that he conceived it as an image lying at its centre, conceived it so intensely that it constantly broke the surface of the verse in which it crystallized, dominating the other images and subduing them to its own great pattern. Thus the theme of *Hamlet* is hinted at by Marcellus – 'Something is rotten in the state of Denmark' – and the imagery is dominated by that of neglect and decay, of disease and 'rank corruption' that 'mining all within, corrupts unseen'. In *Coriolanus* the principal image is introduced by Menenius in the fable of how 'the body's members rebell'd against the belly', and images of the body, its parts and functions, and allied to these, of food and disease, run throughout: 'navel of the state', 'buttock of the night', 'digest things rightly'. In *Antony and Cleopatra* the vast scope of the imperial theme is amplified by the imagery, which consists largely of 'images of the world, the firmament, the ocean and vastness generally',[16] and the note of grandeur is struck at once: Antony is 'the triple pillar of the world', Cleopatra is herself an empire, and time itself is extended when the minutes stretch instead of pass:

> There's not a minute of our lives should stretch
> Without some pleasure now.

Even in the comedies, in which the theme is so much less momentous, and the imagery therefore of less import, Shakespeare has a way of returning to one of the principal images, and by this restatement charging it with a dramatic significance and something of the harmonizing quality of the dominating image of the tragedies. Thus, the first lines

INTRODUCTION

of *Twelfth Night* are those of Orsino, craving for the love of Olivia:

> If music be the food of love, play on;
> Give me excess of it, that, surfeiting,
> The appetite may sicken, and so die.

Then in the last scene Olivia gives him his final answer in terms of his own image:

> If it be aught to the old tune, my lord,
> It is as fat and fulsome to mine ear
> As howling after music.

Again, the undeniably Shakespearean part of Pericles opens to the words of Pericles himself as he addresses the waves that threaten to engulf his ship, and with it his queen and sea-born daughter:

> Thou god of this great vast, rebuke these surges,
> That wash both heaven and hell.

How fitting, therefore, and how moving is the image that he uses when Marina, long lost, is restored to him:

> Give me a gash, put me to present pain,
> Lest this great sea of joys rushing upon me
> O'erbear the shores of my mortality,
> And drown me with their sweetness.

The same unifying and harmonizing principle is often found within the smaller unit of a speech that is of sufficient length and dramatic importance: a restatement of an earlier image, which resolves the intermediate images and brings them within its pattern, as when Ophelia describes Hamlet as 'The expectancy and rose of the fair state', that is, to put it into another Shakespearean idiom, as the promised beauty of the unblown rose, then after the intervening images of mirror and model, honey and music, bells and discord, returns with infinite pathos to the initial image, 'That unmatched form and feature of blown youth Blasted with ecstasy'. Then, consider Prospero's speech when he dismisses the spirits that have performed the Masque of the Three Goddesses:

> Our revels now are ended. These our actors,
> As I foretold you, were all spirits, and
> Are melted into air, into thin air;
> And like the baseless fabric of this vision,
> The cloud-capp'd towers, the gorgeous palaces,
> The solemn temples, the great globe itself,
> Yea, all which it inherit, shall dissolve,
> And, like this insubstantial pageant faded,
> Leave not a rack behind. We are such stuff
> As dreams are made on, and our little life
> Is rounded with a sleep.

In these lines, perhaps the most beautiful that Shakespeare ever wrote, the triple counterpoint of imagery, phrase and rhythm reaches its final perfection. Though metrically almost regular, much of their beauty lies in the counter-rhythm induced by the assonantal sequences of false trochees and related words – *revels, temples; actors, fabric, pageant, baseless* – sequences that are linked by that of the verbs, *ended, melted, faded*, with their remote connotations and fading cadences. The verse must be slowly and deliberately spoken, and full emphasis given to its imposed and falling rhythm, though there are perhaps no other three

INTRODUCTION

words so difficult to speak, because of their sheer beauty, as 'insubstantial pageant faded'. The speech begins with a simple statement, introducing three lines which, by the disproportionate number of words that begin with a vowel, by the fragility of these words and by the slight pause necessitated before speaking them, express something of the heartache at what time has taken away. Then begins the deeper and more solemn music of the development: what time will take away. The theme of finality and dissolution is announced by *ended*, and developed with variations by the other three verbs, *ended* being linked to *rounded* by its rhyming consonants, while the rhythm of 'Are melted into air' is exactly repeated in 'Is rounded with a sleep', so that air and sleep are imaginatively identified with one another and with an enveloping forgetfulness. Then, the central image of the dissolution of the great globe itself, Lear's 'thick rotundity o' the world', is restated, or recalled by the final image, with its antithesis, of the oblivion that lies beyond life's dream, 'our *little* life Is *rounded* with a sleep'.

It is poetry such as this, which, by its perfection of phrase, its musical sequences of words, its imposed and varying rhythms, its illuminating and harmonizing imagery, conveys more than has ever been communicated by any other poet, of the experience, the vision that inspired the writing; it is such poetry – not the learning, not the philosophy, not even the characters, for they are themselves the poetry – that makes the plays of Shakespeare so incomparably the greatest achievement of man's genius.

1   Though sunk in death the forms the Poet drew,
    The actor's genius bade them breathe anew;
    Though, like the bard himself, in night they lay,
    Immortal Garrick call'd them back to day,
    And till eternity with pow'r sublime

The Poetry of Shakespeare's Plays

    Shall mark the mortal hour of hoary Time,
    Shakespeare and Garrick like twin-stars shall shine,
    And earth irradiate with beam divine.

2 I take this opportunity of acknowledging my indebtedness to DR CAROLINE SPURGEON's *Shakespeare's Imagery*.

3 Since this Introduction was written, DR IFOR EVANS has published his *Language of Shakespeare's Plays*.

4 Until Robert Atkins' Old Vic production of 1922 it was customary to cut the play to about half its length and to reduce it to about a dozen scenes, to make room for the changes of sumptuous scenery and the 'splendour of song, dance and procession'.

5 'How, I ask you, are stage-enthusiasts – I ask you, Granville-Barker, and you, too, Desmond MacCarthy, and you, Maurice Baring – going to answer Robertson, Charles Lamb, Hazlitt, Coleridge, Goethe and me? It is really up to you to make a reply; and such a reply to be valid should, I suggest, enumerate first of all the scenes in Shakespeare's plays which are only effective upon the stage, and secondly a record of concrete esthetic experiences, of the rendering of Shakespearean roles by great actors and actresses by which the imaginative impression of these roles has been deepened and enriched.' LOGAN PEARSALL SMITH *On Reading Shakespeare*.

6 WORDSWORTH. 'One *impulse* from a vernal wood.'

7 'I can recommend myself as a guide to places, which, although as hideous as possible, are for an artist a paradise.' VAN GOGH.

8 The subject is complex; a landscape by Monet almost certainly resembles the scene that inspired it, but a landscape by Claude or Poussin was almost as certainly inspired by some stimulus other than the scenes depicted, by something not necessarily a landscape at all. A modern instance that illustrates the point in reverse is the work of Ben Nicholson, whose abstract paintings are mostly inspired by landscapes.

9 If the reader will turn to the dictionary and look up the words that lie between *slim* and *sly* he will find them suggestive.

10 By rhetoric is meant the consciously constructed speech of the orator, full of devices for attracting attention and emphasizing a point, and addressed to the audience as much as to the other characters on the stage. It may, of course, be poetry, but it is not fully dramatic. Nor is pure poetry dramatic, for it is the poet himself speaking.

11 Except for the period of the lyrical plays, in which the amount of rhyming dialogue is high. Rhyme does not encourage the feminine ending, and this seems to have affected the blank verse, in which the proportion of lines with feminine endings is only one in twelve.

12 Examples of light endings taken from this scene of *The Tempest* are:
    For now they are oppress'd with travel, they
    Will not...

INTRODUCTION

> The powers, delaying, not forgetting, have
> Incensed the seas...

Of a weak ending formed by a preposition:

> Their manners are more gentle-kind than of
> Our human generation...

13 There are a few earlier examples; cf *The Merchant of Venice*, I. i: 'Do cream and mantle like a standing pond.'

14 It is worth noting that certain ideas were always associated with particular images, notably flattery with dogs and sweetmeats, and rebellion with a flooded river and clothes:

> Why, what a candy deal of courtesy
> This fawning greyhound then did proffer me!

> We come within our awful banks again,
> And knit our powers to the arm of peace.

15 There is a remarkable example in *Antony and Cleopatra*, remarkable not so much for its lateness as for its development as a conceit. It comes in the last speech of Enobarbus, IV. ix:

> Throw my heart
> Against the flint and hardness of my fault,
> Which, being dried with grief, will break to powder,
> And finish all foul thoughts.

16 C SPURGEON: *Shakespeare's Imagery*, p. 350.

Part Two

EARLY PLAYS AND POEMS

HISTORIES
2 *Henry VI*, 3 *Henry VI*, *Richard III*, 1 *Henry VI*.

POEMS
Venus and Adonis, *The Rape of Lucrece*.

COMEDIES
The Comedy of Errors, *The Taming of the Shrew*, *The Two Gentlemen of Verona*, (*Titus Andronicus*).

CHAPTER ONE

Histories

2 Henry VI, 3 Henry VI, Richard III, 1 Henry VI.

The division of Shakespeare's plays into five periods is bound to be somewhat arbitrary, for the style of one period develops naturally out of its predecessor; transitions are rarely abrupt, and as certain essential qualities are common to all, a distinction may be only a matter of degree, and a characteristic a question of emphasis. Then again, some plays are abnormal, having features that belong to more than one style, and it is even possible that there are passages of revision in the majority of them. Nevertheless, taking into account the subject and the mood in which they were written, both of which give additional distinction to the style, it will be found that characteristics are sufficiently well defined to warrant the division.

Of the early histories, 2 and 3 *Henry VI* and *Richard III* form a well-defined group; the theme is the decline and fall of the House of Lancaster, and the rise and rapid eclipse of that of York; in style they closely resemble one another. 1 *Henry VI* is different; it deals with the struggle against Joan of Arc and the latest phase of the Hundred Years War, and only in parts is it clearly by the same hand as that of the other three. These are pre-eminently the blank-verse plays; prose is confined virtually to the Cade scenes in 2 *Henry VI*, the amount of rhyme is almost negligible, and in no other group is the proportion of blank verse to the total number of lines so high, largely because in no other group is the amount of humour and comic relief so small.

Two salient characteristics of the early verse are artificiality and diffuseness, a major cause of which, particularly in the histories, is the rhetorical tradition. Rhetoric, the art of the orator, the art, that is, of persuasion, was one of the most important subjects taught at the universities in the sixteenth century, and it was inevitable that the playwrights who developed the popular drama, most of them university men, should apply the devices of rhetoric to this new medium of blank verse, which by its repetitive structure of line was a more emphatic means of expression than prose. Speeches, therefore, tended to be long, set declamations directed at the audience, and even in the shorter ones the characters in these early plays appear to be more interested in the audience than in their companions on the stage. The lines would be delivered with the extravagant stylized gestures of the orator, the action suiting the word, the word the action, for the apron stage of the public theatres resembled the orator's platform and encouraged the conception that drama was only another and more exciting form of public oratory.[1] In this rhetorical verse line is piled remorselessly on line, question on question, and illustration on illustration, with little variety, and all the flourishes of rhetoric are displayed to astonish and impress the audience with the oratorical skill of the author. Suffolk's ferocious invective in 2 *Henry VI*, III. ii, is a good example of this, as well as of the hyperbolic language in which emotions are expressed:

> A plague upon them! wherefore should I curse them?
> Would curses kill, as doth the mandrake's groan,
> I would invent as bitter-searching terms,
> As curst, as harsh and horrible to hear,
> Deliver'd strongly through my fixed teeth,
> With full as many signs of deadly hate,
> As lean-faced Envy in her loathsome cave:
> My tongue should stumble in mine earnest words;
> Mine eyes should sparkle like the beaten flint,
> Mine hair be fix'd on end, as one distract;
> Ay, every joint should seem to curse and ban:
> And even now my burthen'd heart would break,
> Should I not curse them. Poison be their drink!
> Gall, worse than gall, the daintiest that they taste!
> Their sweetest shade a grove of cypress trees!
> Their chiefest prospect murdering basilisks!
> Their softest touch as smart as lizards' stings!
> Their music frightful as the serpent's hiss,
> And boding screech-owls make the concert full!

The verse is indistinguishable from that of early Marlowe. The line, both metrically and grammatically, is the unit; each is complete in itself, and as there is no imposed secondary rhythm to give coherence many of them might be transposed or even abstracted with little loss to the meaning, or alternatively the series of parallel and identical constructions might be indefinitely prolonged. All this structural repetition of line and iteration of detail, of phrase, word and even of letter, is a conscious and sonorous elaboration for elaboration's sake, as is the purely verbal wit of the early type of pun:

> Unto the main! O father, Main is lost;
> That Maine which by main force Warwick did win,

And would have kept so long as breath did last!
Main chance, father, you meant; but I meant Maine.

It may be admirable rhetoric, but it is scarcely dramatic verse.

Typical lines are those in which phrase is balanced against phrase, or in which adjectives and nouns are accumulated, and sometimes piled up without conjunctions: 'Of comfort, kingdom, kindred, freedom, life.' Other characteristics of this early verse are the compound epithets: 'bitter-searching terms', 'pretty-vaulting sea'; Latin quotations, as when the young Rutland dies with a line of Ovid on his lips; antithesis: 'an outward honour for an inward woe' (a good example of the balanced line); aphorism – for the didacticism of the Senecan drama is powerful in these plays – frequently in terms of the elements or of animals:

A little fire is quickly trodden out;
Which, being suffer'd, rivers cannot quench.

Stichomythia, or line-by-line dialogue, another Senecan legacy, is particularly common in quarrel scenes, of which the plays are full, and is generally in normal blank verse, but there are experiments in a shorter line, as in *Richard III*, I.ii:

Anne. I would I knew thy heart.
Glou. 'Tis figured in my tongue.
Anne. I fear me both are false.
Glou. Then never man was true...

Buckingham's line, 'Trust nobody, for fear you be betrayed', summarizes the cynical brutality of 2 *Henry VI*, but the third part is even more cynical and more brutal. A cumulatively depressive effect is brought about by the appalling characters who, with the exception of the king, are impelled only by selfishness, and act only in a ruthless struggle for power. Margaret is a she-wolf, an Amazonian trull with a vizard-like unchanging countenance, and Richard a foul misshapen stigmatic, while lascivious Edward, perjured George, wind-changing Warwick, child-killer Clifford, and the rest of the liars, braggarts, bullies and assassins are little better. This lack of variety in the characters is fatally unrelieved by other forms of variety. There is no prose, no humour, and there is little poetry. In 2 *Henry VI* there is the relief of the prose scenes in which Mr Masefield too seriously finds 'more sadness and horror of heart than humour', and the two great poets, Shakespeare and Marlowe, 'brooding together on life', and there is the poetry of the love scenes between Suffolk and Margaret. In *Richard III*, Gloucester has developed a Shakespearean and most unMarlovian sense of humour, but in 3 *Henry VI* there is none of these things. As a result the rhetoric is more frequently overwrought and degenerates into fustian, and if Tolstoy's stricture that all Shakespeare's characters speak the same language, and a language that never could be spoken by men, were confined to this play, there would be some justification for it. For example, Richard tells Warwick:

If this right hand would buy two hours' life,
That I in all despite might rail at him,
This hand should chop it off, and with the issuing blood
Stifle the villain, whose unstanched thirst
York and young Rutland could not satisfy.

Evidently Warwick was impressed, for later when he is on the other side he defies Richard:

The Poetry of Shakespeare's Plays

> I had rather chop this hand off at a blow,
> And with the other fling it at thy face,
> Than bear so low a sail, to strike to thee.

The imagery may be regarded either as an unconscious reflection or as a deliberate intensification of the pitiless and adamantine theme. An atmosphere of heartlessness and cruelty is suggested by the constantly recurring images from flint, snakes, beasts of prey, and the butchery of animals, and even the so-Shakespearean allusions to birds and gardens are often used with sinister effect, the lime twigs, like the web of the labouring spider, being traps. Then in 3 *Henry VI* another image is developed, which contributes not a little to the oppressiveness of the play: that of the sun, its parching and shrivelling power, and the subsidiary image of fire. Dr Spurgeon has shown that the 'conception of the king as sun is fairly constant with Shakespeare', but here it is something more; it is a pitiless, burning sun, from whose rays there is no protection, no shadow, no relief, a bloody sun in a hot and copper sky. The image is introduced by Margaret:

> What, hath thy fiery heart so parch'd thine entrails
> That not a tear can fall for Rutland's death?

And then the 'summer's scalding heat' runs through the rest of the play. The atmosphere of sterility and destruction is almost perversely intensified by the image of the plant uprooted with the murdering knife, and the tree chopped down with the axe. Even the sea imagery, of which there is an abnormal amount, and which might have been expected to afford some relief, serves the same purpose, culminating in the elaborate forty-line conceit of Margaret's address to

EARLY PLAYS AND POEMS

her troops at Tewkesbury, in which Edward is a ruthless sea, Clarence a quicksand, and Richard a ragged fatal rock.

There are, however, occasional oases amid this sickening desolation, when Shakespeare, instead of a perfunctory reference to a wolf or tiger, introduces an image from his own observation of nature or country life:

> Their weapons like to lightning came and went;
> Our soldiers', like the night owl's lazy flight,
> Or like an idle thresher with a flail,
> Fell gently down, as if they struck their friends.

And before the battle of Towton, King Henry in his moving lyrical soliloquy perfectly expresses the longing for the cool and soothing refuge afforded by nature: for the sweet shade of a hawthorn-bush, and the shepherd's cold thin drink out of his leather bottle.

The change of atmosphere from the last two parts of *Henry VI* to *Richard III* is remarkable. After the fever and aridity of the one we breathe a fresher and more liberal air; the torrid summer's scalding heat has become the glorious summer of a more temperate clime; the hard glare has been reduced to luminosity, and the tawny scene has assumed softer and more various tones and hues. This is surprising when we consider the dominating character of Richard – for *Richard III* without the Duke of Gloucester is as absurd as *Hamlet* without the Prince of Denmark – who might so easily have outstrutted and outfretted his father, York, and forced the whole play on to the flat and monotonous plane of his rhetoric. Melodramatic Gloucester may be, but he is never monotonous; declamatory he can be, but he is rarely tedious, for he combines the poetry of Marlowe with the poetry and humour of Shakespeare.

The Poetry of Shakespeare's Plays

It is this Shakespearean grace of humour that accounts partly for the difference. But it is not alone the humour, the presence of a number of innocent and kindly people, and the more complex characterization that add variety and therefore interest to the play; nor is it the slight technical advance in the verse so much as a greater ease and flexibility of expression. In *Richard III* Shakespeare is no longer a beginner straining at language and forcing it to an unnatural pitch of intensity; he is confident, almost colloquial at times, and prepared to take liberties and risks. It is this ease, this confidence, that gives the play a liveliness that distinguishes it from the preceding parts of the tetralogy. Though the writing is unequal, and in a set scene or speech the verse still creaks somewhat under its load of rhetorical contrivances, there are passages where Shakespeare forgets Marlowe and the grand style, and slips into the simpler and more natural idiom that anticipates the triumphs of his later plays:

> He cannot live, I hope; and must not die,
> Till George be pack'd with post-horse up to heaven.
> I'll in, to urge his hatred more to Clarence,
> With lies well steel'd with weighty arguments;
> And, if I fail not in my deep intent,
> Clarence hath not another day to live:
> Which done, God take King Edward to his mercy,
> And leave the world for me to bustle in.

There is nothing quite like this in 2 and 3 *Henry VI*.

Henry VI Part One is different again. There can be little doubt that most of it is the work of an inferior dramatist, and it seems probable that after writing the trilogy of the Wars of the Roses, Shakespeare adapted an old play that dealt with the early years of Henry VI to serve as an introduction. That the adaptation is later than the other three parts is suggested by the subtler rhythm of the verse in the Temple Garden scene (II. iv), and by the restraint of the writing, in which a new lyricism takes the place of the old fustian:

> *Plan.* Meantime your cheeks do counterfeit our roses;
> For pale they look with fear, as witnessing
> The truth on our side.
>   *Som.*   No, Plantagenet,
> 'Tis not for fear but anger that thy cheeks
> Blush for pure shame to counterfeit our roses,
> And yet thy tongue will not confess thy error.
>   *Plan.* Hath not thy rose a canker, Somerset?
>   *Som.* Hath not thy rose a thorn, Plantagenet?
>   *Plan.* Ay, sharp and piercing, to maintain his truth;
> Whiles thy consuming canker eats his falsehood.
>   *Som.* Well, I'll find friends to wear my bleeding roses…

Of course this lyrical note is not altogether new; the novelty lies in finding it in a quarrel scene, and we can trace its origin in the earliest histories. There the characteristic poetic line is an arrogant alliterative one, often incorporating an architectural or heraldic allusion, or a reference to conquest, as in 'Defacing monuments of conquer'd France'; but sometimes the balanced and percussive rhetorical line modulates into a more musical one harmonized by the vowels:

> To watch the coming of my punish'd duchess.
> Lest, being suffer'd in that harmful slumber.
> Which in their summer beauty kissed each other.

Such lines, with their central and final verbal trochees assonantally related, are characteristic of Shakespeare's next phase. They are brilliantly exploited by Gloucester in his first speech in *Richard III*: 'Cheated of feature by dissembling nature'; and again:

> And now, instead of mounting barbed steeds
> To fright the souls of fearful adversaries,
> He capers nimbly in a lady's chamber
> To the lascivious pleasing of a lute.

The varied measure of lines like these, sometimes gaily, sometimes elegiacally employed, is beyond the range of Marlowe's achievement, and is as unmistakably Shakespearean as the verse of *Hamlet*. Then, it is in the least poetical of these early plays, 3 *Henry VI*, that Shakespeare protests against the brutality of the Wars of the Roses, and writes from his heart the lines that prefigure the poet of the *Sonnets* and *Romeo and Juliet*:

> See how the morning opes her golden gates,
> And takes her farewell of the glorious sun!
> How well resembles it the prime of youth,
> Trimm'd like a younker prancing to his love!

---

1 It is probable that in the private theatres occupied by the boys' companies both declamation and gesture were less extravagant. *Hamlet* was written at a time when the competition of the boys was hitting the adult companies hard, and in Hamlet's advice to the players Shakespeare seems to be demonstrating the more natural style of acting that he had taught his company. The Player's speech on Hecuba is delivered in the old manner, and Hamlet criticizes it later when he begs the actor not to mouth his lines, and not to saw the air too much with his hand.

CHAPTER TWO

Poems

Venus and Adonis, The Rape of Lucrece.

These two poems are essential reading for the full appreciation of the plays that Shakespeare was writing at about the same period, for they are the link between the declamation of the early histories and the modified rhetoric of the early comedies and lyrical plays. Polonius would have described them rightly as lyrical-rhetorical. They are two of the most extravagantly elaborate and artificial poems in the language, academic exercises in dialectics heavily overlaid with exuberant Renaissance ornament. The one is essentially a fine-spun and teasingly ingenious argument in favour of illicit love, the other an equally dexterous and unconvincing argument against it. However, they were very much in the fashion of the day as set by Spenser and Marlowe, and clearly it was not easy for a poet saturated in such a tradition to exclude their undramatic excesses from his plays when he turned to the stage for his livelihood; then, they were exceedingly popular, particularly the first, that 'luscious marrowbone pie', and the temptation to exploit their success must have been correspondingly strong; but though their influence is everywhere apparent it is never overwhelming, and the remarkable thing is not the profusion of rhetoric in the early histories and of far-fetched conceit in the comedies, but the moderation with which Shakespeare employed them.

Coleridge appears to have been the first critic to have remarked that Shakespeare was a poet before he was a dramatist, that 'previously to his appearance as a dramatic poet... Shakespeare possessed the chief, if not every, requisite of a poet'. In *Venus and Adonis* he showed that he possessed deep feeling, an exquisite sense of beauty both of form and sound, a love of nature, and the faculty of projecting himself into the object of his contemplation. Moreover, he possessed fancy, 'considered as the faculty of bringing together images dissimilar in the main by some one point or more of likeness'; he possessed imagination, 'the power by which one image or feeling is made to modify many others, and by a sort of fusion to force many into one'; and finally 'in this poem and the *Rape of Lucrece*, Shakespeare gave ample proof of his possession of a most profound, energetic, and philosophical mind, without which he might have pleased, but could not have been a great dramatic poet'.

On the other hand Hazlitt, who was always delighted to disagree with Coleridge, even to the spelling of Shakespeare's name, replied: 'It has been the fashion of late to cry up our auther's poems as equal to his plays: this is the desperate cant of modern criticism. We would ask, was there the slightest comparison between Shakespear, and either Chaucer and Spenser, as mere poets? Not any. The two poems of Venus and Adonis and of Tarquin and Lucrece appear to us like a couple of ice-houses. They are about as hard, as glittering, and as cold.'

Coleridge was probably being wise after the event; 'had no Lear, no Othello, no Henry IV, no Twelfth Night ever appeared' it is to be doubted if he would have found as much as he professed to find in *Venus and Adonis*; Hazlitt was being more than usually perverse, and had Coleridge not written he might have found more to admire.

And yet it is easy to see why Hazlitt was chilled by the poem. Ostensibly the theme is passionate – what could be more passionate than the Goddess of Love herself making love? – but Shakespeare, though he projected himself sympathetically into the hare and the snail, either failed or made little attempt to project his mind into that of Venus. But then neither the hare nor the snail takes part in the debate. Venus speaks passionate words, but her creator is himself so dispassionately Olympian, so engrossed with her intricate dialectic, that there is no fire, no heat, no pain in what she says. Shakespeare is in Byzantium, the city of artifice, of hammered gold and gold enamelling,

> Where blood-begotten spirits come
> And all complexities of fury leave.

All, or almost all, is as far removed from reality as possible. The story itself is taken from classical mythology, the six-line stanza is rigid with rhetorical constructions and studded with compound and decorative epithets. The diction, too, is studiously artificial and 'poetical': the tongue is 'the heart's attorney' or 'the engine of her thoughts'; the mouth 'a ruby-coloured portal'; lips wear crimson liveries; eyes are 'two blue windows'; tears are 'orient drops'; the sun is 'the world's comforter', and the lark's nest 'his moist cabinet'. Colours are for the most part the bright and vivid hues of heraldry, the simple abstractions and intense symbols of childhood. Thus, as for the child all vegetation is green, tree-trunks brown, and sky blue, so according to the Elizabethan convention the skin and teeth are white, lips red, hair gold, and veins blue. Red and white are the predominating colours in Shakespeare's early poetry: thus, in the second stanza Venus describes Adonis as 'More white and red than doves or roses are'; she herself has 'lily fingers', her arms are 'an ivory pale', and

> Full gently now she takes him by the hand,
> A lily prison'd in a gaol of snow,
> Or ivory in an alabaster band.

Red and white are the colours symbolic not only of physical beauty, but of emotional states and spiritual qualities as well; shame and love are red, anger and fear are white, and Adonis lours and frets ''Twixt crimson shame, and anger ashy-pale'.

Most of the imagery is equally unnatural:

> Here overcome, as one full of despair,
> She vail'd her eyelids, who, like sluices, stopp'd
> The crystal tide that from her two cheeks fair
> In the sweet channel of her bosom dropp'd;
> > But through the flood-gates breaks the silver rain,
> > And with his strong course opens them again...

and so on for two more stanzas. This is scarcely the product of imagination, a spontaneous fusion of object and image, scarcely even is it fancy, considered as the faculty of bringing together images dissimilar in the main by some one point or more of likeness. It is a forcing together not only of similarities but of dissimilarities as well, an attempt to make object and image agree with one another at all points. Then such a method, a succession of relative clauses each developing out of its predecessor, might be pursued indefinitely. A few years later Falstaff was to make fun of this kind of writing:

> For God's sake, lords, convey my tristful queen,
> For tears do stop the flood-gates of her eyes,

and the world of difference between early conceit and mature metaphor may be appreciated by comparing the use of the image in *Venus and Adonis* with that in *Othello*:

> for my particular grief
> Is of so flood-gate and o'erbearing nature
> That it engluts and swallows other sorrows.

The thought is as artfully elaborated as the imagery. Never has goddess or woman wooed with such perverse ingenuity and pedantic persistency, and it is little wonder that Adonis is unmoved by the sententious rhetoric of the love-sick and sweating queen:

> Seeds spring from seeds and beauty breedeth beauty;
> Thou wast begot; to get it is thy duty.

Venus' apostrophe to Death is only one of the ornamental digressions with which the poem is so heavily loaded. Even the famous description of Adonis' horse reminds one less of a real horse than of a metal monument by Verrocchio or Donatello, and the fatal boar itself is no more dangerous than a Renaissance bronze.

Yet among these bronzes, these plump and painted plaster figures, a baroque tableau set in an enamelled landscape, there are simple touches of nature that stand out with startling clarity and incongruous beauty. Through the veneer of sophistication we catch glimpses of the poet who still thought of Stratford as his home, and remembered nostalgically the countryside where he and nature had been long acquainted. Though his description of the gentle lark mounting from his moist cabinet is somewhat conventionally worked out in a succession of dependent clauses, there is nothing bookish about the image inspired by Adonis' shyness:

> Upon this promise did he raise his chin,
> Like a dive-dapper peering through a wave,
> Who, being looked on, ducks as quickly in,

or about the daringly humble one descriptive of Venus' quick withdrawal of her eyes when she sees the body of the dead Adonis:

> Or as the snail, whose tender horns being hit,
> Shrinks backward in his shelly cave with pain,
> And there all smother'd up in shade doth sit,
> Long after fearing to creep forth again.[1]

Then, the most famous of the digressions is the description of the hunted hare, strangely and undramatically put into the mouth of Venus, who tries to persuade Adonis to hunt something less dangerous than a boar. Here, for five or six stanzas Shakespeare forgets his classical models and returns in thought to the scenes of his boyhood. Though in one sense it is undramatic, in another, because it is a reflection of life and not of art, it may be claimed as the most dramatic, perhaps the only dramatic, passage in the poem.

Lucrece is as far removed from reality as *Venus and Adonis*; the successful rape is every whit as pedantic as the frustrated seduction, and Lucrece and Tarquin display even greater virtuosity as rhetoricians than Venus and Adonis. The hundred-line disputation between Tarquin's frozen conscience and hot-burning will is followed by an academic debate of twice the length between the ravisher and his helpless victim, and it is not without sympathy from the reader that Tarquin puts an end to the delicately balanced antitheses and oxymorons of Lucrece's arguments. The rape, however, is only an episode, a temporary check that merely deflects the current of her rhetoric, and an occasion for her three-hundred-line apostrophes to Night, Opportunity and Time, which are the centre and kernel of the poem. There is no real passion in the lines, her declamation is the expression of an unfelt sorrow, and conceit, a stretched and twisted thought, is a substitute for pain. Though her death is dramatically contrived, coming with unexpected swiftness after the long delay, there is nothing in the poem to suggest that the author would be more than a commonplace dramatist if he turned his talents to the stage.

The verse is a shade less artificial than that of *Venus and Adonis*, though the dazzling description of the sleeping Lucrece is a classical example of the whole range of Elizabethan emblematic imagery:

Her lily hand her rosy cheek lies under...

Without the bed her other fair hand was,
On the green coverlet; whose perfect white
Show'd like an April daisy on the grass,
With pearly sweat, resembling dew of night.
Her eyes, like marigolds, had sheathed their light,
    And canopied in darkness sweetly lay,
    Till they might open to adorn the day.

Her hair, like golden threads, play'd with her breath...
Her breasts, like ivory globes circled with blue...
    Her azure veins, her alabaster skin,
    Her coral lips, her snow-white dimpled chin.

The Poetry of Shakespeare's Plays

Even here, however, in the rhythm and harmony of the line, 'Show'd like an April daisy on the grass', we can detect the music of the next phase; and though the simile is as conventional as the others, it falls with a Chaucerian sweetness and freshness and an unaffected simplicity. Then again, in the high-piled rhetoric of Lucrece's address to Time there are lines that have the stately measure and sonorous diction of the *Sonnets*:

> Time's glory is to calm contending kings,
> To unmask falsehood and bring truth to light,
> To stamp the seal of time in aged things...
>   To ruinate proud buildings with thy hours,
>   And smear with dust their glittering golden towers;
>
> To fill with worm-holes stately monuments,
> To feed oblivion with decay of things,
> To blot old books and alter their contents...
>   To spoil antiquities of hammer'd steel,
>   And turn the giddy round of Fortune's wheel.

Even Tarquin speaks three lines that have their peculiar and piercing vernal quality:

> Like little frosts that sometime threat the spring,
> To add a more rejoicing to the prime,
> And give the sneaped birds more cause to sing.

And once at least the full glory of the sonnet poetry breaks through the heavily encrusted verse:

> As is the morning's silver-melting dew
> Against the golden splendour of the sun.

Venus and Adonis and *Lucrece* are the product of an age of transition and confusion lying between the old order of the Middle Ages and the new order of the seventeenth century. The medieval organization had broken down, and when Shakespeare began to write, England had not yet found a solution to its problems, social, political, religious, and artistic. The new civilization of the Renaissance was being grafted on what remained of the old, and the operation was not yet complete; it was an age of empiricism, of trial and error, of violent and adventurous experiment, when men did not fully understand their new materials. We can see this in the visual arts of the period, particularly in architecture, where buildings still essentially Gothic are sometimes encumbered with classical ornament immoderately misapplied. It is not that they are pretentious, or that the ornament is meretricious; on the contrary they are often very beautiful; it is simply that the relation between classical structure and classical ornament was not fully understood, that the one without the other loses much of its significance.

These early poems resemble one of these buildings; they are medieval in their loose and rambling structure, their wayward and leisurely development, their prolixity and didacticism, but in their ornament they are overwhelmingly of the Renaissance, and by their shameless exuberance may offend a puritanical taste. We live in an age mistrustful of ornament, and apt to condemn it as non-functional and otiose, but in Shakespeare's time there were new words as well as new worlds to conquer, and verbal exploration and experiment were almost as exciting as geographical and scientific discovery. For those who enjoy ornament for its own sake, who appreciate fancy as well as imagination, and take pleasure in the yoking together by violence of the most heterogeneous ideas, who, in short, like their art quite frankly to be art and as far removed from nature as possible, for those there is poetry in plenty, poetry, in the words of Adonis, ' bewitching like the wanton mermaid's songs'.

---

1 It was with reference to this simile that Keats wrote, 'He has left nothing to say about nothing or anything'. Shakespeare uses the same figure in *Love's Labour's Lost*, IV. iii. 334, and more than a decade later it reappears in *Coriolanus*, IV. vi. 43, in the form of a metaphor.

CHAPTER THREE

Comedies

The Comedy of Errors, The Taming of the Shrew, The Two Gentlemen of Verona, (*Titus Andronicus*).

The plays of this group are both transitional and experimental. Shakespeare abandons Holinshed and English history for the greater freedom of fiction, and taking his material from classical and renaissance Europe, from Plautus, Seneca, Ovid, Ariosto, and Montemayor, produces two farces, a romantic comedy, and a tragedy of revenge. Experiment in genre involved experiment in medium. Apart from the Cade and Horner scenes in 2 *Henry VI*, and these are by no means all humorous, he had not yet tried his hand at comedy, so that after the blank verse of the histories he had to find a suitable vehicle for his new venture. This problem he solved, temporarily at least, by keeping blank verse as the staple medium, to be spoken by the more serious characters; for low comedy he varied prose with the doggerel of the old farces like *Ralf Roister Doister*, to courtly comedy and love passages he added the ornament of rhyme, and *The Two Gentlemen of Verona* contains the first of his lyrics. Doggerel, however, is confined to the three comedies of this group and *Love's Labour's Lost*, the first of the next, for clearly this sort of stuff, though high-spirited and not without charm, will not do for anything but trivialities:

> Say what you will, sir, but I know what I know;
> That you beat me at the mart, I have your hand to show:
> If the skin were parchment, and the blows you gave were ink,
> Your own handwriting would tell you what I think.

In technique the blank verse is deceptively similar to that of the histories; there is comparatively little modification of rhythm by variation of stress and pause, and the self-contained and end-stopped line remains the dominating structural and melodic unit. The more violent passages are constructed after the old rhetorical, cumulative pattern: thus, when Adriana mistakes Antipholus of Syracuse for her husband and charges him with infidelity, she unpacks her heart with words for all the world like Queen Margaret in *Henry VI*:

> Wouldst thou not spit at me and spurn at me,
> And hurl the name of husband in my face,
> And tear the stain'd skin off my harlot brow,
> And from my false hand cut the wedding ring...

Even Aegeon's moving appeal for recognition in the last scene of *The Comedy of Errors*, 'O, grief hath changed me since you saw me last', is too rhetorical to be fully dramatic, and lines like the splendid,

> What fool hath added water to the sea,
> Or brought a faggot to bright-burning Troy?

have the hard brilliance that we associate with the histories. Proteus echoes their rhetorical Euphuism, and Julia sometimes speaks the enamelled language of *Venus and Adonis*.

Original and arresting images are relatively few; most of them are ornamental rather than illustrative, many of them lengthy, typically in the form of a simile, sometimes expanded into a conceit, and, however beautiful, they may have little to do with the play, as when Julia invents a sonnet-long allegory of a stream, in defence of her decision to follow Proteus. It is enchanting poetry, but it is not dramatic poetry, for its pace bears no relation to that of the action, which is held up while Shakespeare speaks lyric in the person of his heroine. Nor, we may feel, is it dramatic to give Proteus, the first of the long line of caddish heroes, so much of the finest poetry. Though we cannot help resenting this, it is characteristic of Shakespeare's careless tolerance and impartiality, but it may be that he was deliberately doing for Proteus what he later did for his vicious tragic heroes and protagonists, for King John and Claudius, giving him his own bewitching language to prevent the complete alienation of our sympathies and suspension of our belief in the story, for after all, this young gentleman of Verona is beloved of Julia, the first and not the least charming of his romantic heroines. And then, he makes Proteus apologize both for himself and his successors, for Claudio, Bertram, and the rest:

> O heaven, were man
> But constant, he were perfect! That one error
> Fills him with faults; makes him run through all the sins.

But despite the rhetoric, the fragments of fustian, the over-literary artifice, and other undramatic excesses and excursions, an encroaching naturalism is to be detected in these plays. Petruchio parodies the encrusted language of *Lucrece* when in his lines he pretends that old Vincentio is a young woman:

> Such war of white and red within her cheeks!
> What stars do spangle heaven with such beauty,
> As those two eyes become that heavenly face?

and half ironically, half affectionately, he describes Kate in terms of the simplest natural objects:

> Kate, like the hazel-twig
> Is straight and slender, and as brown in hue
> As hazel-nuts and sweeter than the kernels.

And in *Titus Andronicus*, a play with a plot even more uncompromisingly ferocious than those of the early histories, there is a surprising amount of nature imagery, lyrically and not vituperatively employed. Then the episode in *The Two Gentlemen*, IV. ii, in which Julia overhears her lover's perfidy and the night-music to Silvia – like so many of Shakespeare's lyrics, an effortless composition based on the letters *s,i,e* – and her subsequent dark dialogue with Proteus, are Shakespeare's first dramatically successful passages of romantic pathos:

> *Pro.* Go presently, and take this ring with thee,
> Deliver it to Madam Silvia:
> She lov'd me well, deliver'd it to me.
>   *Jul.* It seems you loved not her, to leave her token.
> She is dead belike?
>   *Pro.* Not so; I think she lives.
>   *Jul.* Alas!

It reminds one irresistibly of Viola's confession to Orsino, and her question, 'She is dead, belike?' has something of the same thrilling quality as Viola's, 'What think you, sailors?'

This lyrical note becomes progressively more assertive, but it is not the result only of the greater naturalism of diction and imagery; it is in the verse as a whole. The earliest verse is essentially a succession of self-contained lines rhetorically related, but now the relationship becomes increasingly a much more subtle one of verbal harmony. Consider the speech of the Lord in the second scene of *The Taming of the Shrew*:

> Wilt thou have music? hark! Appollo plays,
> And twenty caged nightingales do sing:
> Or wilt thou sleep? we'll have thee to a couch
> Softer and sweeter than the lustful bed
> On purpose trimm'd up for Semiramis.
> Say thou wilt walk; we will bestrew the ground:
> Or wilt thou ride? thy horses shall be trapp'd,
> Their harness studdied all with gold and pearl.
> Dost thou love hawking? thou hast hawks will soar
> Above the morning lark: or wilt thou hunt?
> Thy hounds shall make the welkin answer them,
> And fetch shrill echoes from the hollow earth.

It is true that the rhetorical structure is very pronounced here, and the verse exceptionally flexible for the period, but the chief harmonizing element is in the words themselves, in the assonantal sequences, *hark, walk, hawk, lark*; *horses, harness, hawking, morning*; *Apollo, echo, hollow*. The last group is very characteristic of Shakespeare, and a similar sequence will be found in Tamora's speech in *Titus Andronicus* II. iii, beginning, 'The birds chant melody on every bush', where we have *shadow, echo, yellow, Dido, melodious.* It is almost as though this speech served unconsciously as a model for others in the later plays, for the celestial duet in *The Merchant of Venice*, with its *shadow...Dido with a willow*, and Gertrude's elegy in *Hamlet*, *willow grows...melodious*, and it is worth remarking that Viola recalls Tamora's 'babbling echo' when she speaks of 'the babbling gossip of the air' in a passage that contains *willow, halloo*, and other related words.

The earliest example of this extension of the harmony from the line to the passage as a whole is in *The Comedy of Errors*, III. ii, where Antipholus of Syracuse makes love to the bewildered Luciana. His speech is in alternate rhyme, and the assonance is emphasized by fixing it on trochaic words that immediately precede or succeed the middle of the line:

Than our earth's wonder; more than earth divine...
To make it wander in an unknown field.

It is all very self-conscious and unashamedly undramatic – Shakespeare has forgotten the play in the excitement of the poetry – but it is a development of profound significance.

In *The Two Gentlemen of Verona* assonance has been pushed much further than a simple sequence of related syllables, and sometimes approaches the complex and concentrated pattern of internal rhyme that reaches its full perfection in *The Merchant of Venice*, as when Valentine meditates on Silvia:

O thou that dost inhabit in my *breast*,
Leave not the mansion *so* long tenant*less*,
*Lest, grow*ing ruinous, the building fall,
And *leave no* memory of what it was.

And again, when he tells Proteus that Julia

> shall be dignified with this high honour, –
> To bear my *lady's train, lest the* base earth
> Should from her *vesture* chance to steal a *kiss*,
> And, of so *great a favour* growing proud,
> *Disdain* to root the summer-swelling flower,
> And make rough winter everlastingly.

The last speech illustrates yet another development. It has already been observed that such a line as Richard III's, 'He capers nimbly in a lady's chamber', containing two or more trochaic words, one of which forms a feminine ending, is characteristic of these early comedies. The additional syllable of the feminine ending in itself imparts a falling cadence to the line, but this is emphasized and extended by another verbal trochee placed in juxtaposition, or related to it by assonance. In this way a dropping trochaic measure is imposed on the rising iambic one without any variation of the foot, and rhythmical variety induced without any metrical irregularity. To these early comedies, therefore, the regular end-stopped line with its slow and falling cadence adds a peculiar music:

> Upon a gathered lily almost withered.
> A woman moved is like a fountain troubled.
> To furnish me upon my longing journey.

Valentine has a similar line, but in his speech the process has been taken a stage further, and the rhythmical variation carried beyond the line in which there is an accumulation of verbal trochees to embrace a whole passage. A reversed rhythm is first imparted by the final syllable of *honour*, and because this is echoed in *vesture* a corresponding movement is suggested in the third line, and again in the fourth, where *favour* is reinforced by *great a* and *growing*; then reaching its full development in the triple trochaics of *summer-swelling flower*, it is prolonged in the centrally placed *winter ever*. There is scarcely any irregularity in the verse, and yet by the assonantal relationship of the principal trochaic words another rhythm is woven into the primary one. And not only does the assonance extend and emphasize the secondary rhythm, the rhythm emphasizes the assonance which harmonizes the whole. It is the beginning of the Shakespearean counterpoint that was to transform the rigid pentameter line of blank verse into the most flexible and musical of mediums, and this is why it was said above that in technique the blank verse of the early comedies is *deceptively* similar to that of the histories.

The most beautiful example of this new lyric poetry, which appears so suddenly to have burgeoned during the writing of *The Two Gentlemen of Verona*, is Proteus' advice to Thurio to tangle Silvia's desires by wailful sonnets and heaven-bred poesy:

> Say that upon the altar of her beauty
> You sacrifice your tears, your sighs, your heart...
> For Orpheus' lute was strung with poets' sinews,
> Whose golden touch could soften steel and stones,
> Make tigers tame, and huge leviathans
> Forsake unsounded deeps to dance on sands.
> After your dire-lamenting elegies,
> Visit by night your lady's chamber-window
> With some sweet consort...the night's dead silence
> Will well become such sweet-complaining grievance.

It is Proteus again who delivers the rhyming splendour of,

> O, how this spring of love resembleth
> The uncertain glory of an April day,
> Which now shows all the beauty of the sun,
> And by and by a cloud takes all away!

This, however, is another music: the princely measure of the *Sonnets*.

Part Three

SONNETS AND LYRICAL PLAYS

*Love's Labour's Lost, Romeo and Juliet, Richard II,
A Midsummer Night's Dream, King John, The
Merchant of Venice.*

Although Shakespeare was to write far greater dramatic poetry, he never excelled the pure poetry of the plays of these years in which his lyric genius so rapidly flowered and reached perfection. In all probability they were written over the same period as that in which the majority of the *Sonnets* were composed, and this no doubt accounts for their most obvious characteristic, the high proportion of rhyming dialogue, at least in the first four. In *Love's Labour's Lost* the proportion of pentameter rhyme to pentameter verse as a whole is 62 per cent, in *A Midsummer Night's Dream* 43 per cent, and in *Romeo and Juliet* and *Richard II* nearly 20 per cent, making an average of 35 per cent. *King John* and *The Merchant of Venice* with only 5 per cent do not share this characteristic, but in style they have much more in common with these plays than with the middle comedies and histories in which prose preponderates, *King John*, like *Richard II*, having no prose at all. As the proportion of rhyme to verse in the plays that preceded and succeeded them is only 7 per cent and 4 per cent respectively, it is clear that these so-called lyrical plays form a very distinct group.

Rhyming dialogue is exceptional in Elizabethan drama, so that in these plays we can see Shakespeare experimenting with rhyme as a medium for comedy, tragedy, and history, and then abandoning it as too artificial, in favour of the greater ease and naturalness, the greater dramatic potentialities, therefore, of blank verse. Every variety of rhyme is tried: doggerel, and the snip, snap, quick and home of stichomythia in grotesque anapaestics, though in *Love's*

The Poetry of Shakespeare's Plays

Labour's Lost only, which is much the most wildly experimental:

> Will you prick't with your knife?
> No point, with my knife.
> Now, God save thy life!

Alternate rhyme competes with octosyllabic and heroic couplets, which sometimes have a strangely satirical Augustan flavour:

> This is the ape of form, monsieur the nice,
> That, when he plays at tables, chides the dice.

Biron speaks sonnet, as do Romeo and Juliet in their love-making; even the Bastard Faulconbridge talks in the *Venus and Adonis* stanza, and in it Benvolio is sententious, Paris elegiacal, and the moralizing Escalus concludes the lovers' story.

Perhaps, however, the plays were not so much an experiment in medium as a deliberate exercise in a new form, the lyrical drama, a poem in dramatic form, as *Henry V* was later to be an experiment in epic drama, and we can imagine Shakespeare wondering whether to follow Arthur Brooke and write a poem on 'The Tragicall Historye of Romeus and Juliet' in the manner of *Lucrece,* or like the unknown author of the old play to set forth the same argument on the stage. In any event these rhyming plays, in which the detail so often obscures the whole, and the manner overwhelms the matter, in which the poetry, rhymed or unrhymed, is so often unrelated to character and action, or at least character and action are lightly sacrificed to poetry, and even to a quibble if there is any occasion for conflict, are dramatic poems almost as much as they are poetic drama.

To take a not extreme example: consider the speech of the bustling and cynical Bolingbroke when he captures Richard at Flint Castle (*Richard II*, III. iii):

> Methinks King Richard and myself should meet
> With no less terror than the elements
> Of fire and water, when their thundering shock
> At meeting tears the cloudy cheeks of heaven.
> Be he the fire, I'll be the yielding water:
> The rage be his, whilst on the earth I rain
> My waters; on the earth, and not on him.
> See, see, King Richard doth himself appear,
> As doth the blushing discontented sun
> From out the fiery portal of the east,
> When he perceives the envious clouds are bent
> To dim his glory and to stain the track
> Of his bright passage to the occident.

He develops two conceits: the first out of a hyperbolical metaphor, the second by a series of phrases and clauses out of a splendid though conventional king-sun image cast in the form of a simile. Nothing could be more unlike the hard-headed Bolingbroke with his contempt for Richard and his poetry, but nothing could be more like Shakespeare, who must have written Sonnet 33 at about this time:

> Full many a glorious morning have I seen
> Flatter the mountain-tops with sovereign eye,
> Kissing with golden face the meadows green,
> Gilding pale streams with heavenly alchemy;
> Anon permit the basest clouds to ride
> With ugly rack on his celestial face,
> And from the forlorn world his visage hide,
> Stealing unseen to west with this disgrace.

The Poetry of Shakespeare's Plays

These plays, particularly the first three, reverberate with the sonnet poetry, and this is the sonnet whose echo is most often heard; the image was a favourite with Shakespeare, and morning is one of the most insistent themes in the sequence, a theme developed out of its essential subject, time and beauty. The periods of the day and the seasons of the year occur again and again, sometimes in their literal sense, but generally as symbols of age or the passage of time in the cycle of man's life. Swift-footed time is the devourer of the wide world's fading sweets, and Shakespeare feels a great pity for men and women by 'Time's fell hand defaced', a great compassion for beauty 'with Time's injurious hand crushed and o'erworn'. Time and its cruel destructive power, its slow sapping of beauty, is the melancholy inspiration of much of Shakespeare's poetry. But when he wrote the *Sonnets* he was a young man in love with the beauty of this delightful world; in them 'beauty' is a word always managed with astonishing freshness and sincerity, and it is not a desolate and faded beauty, but beauty in its prime that leaves the most powerful impression. It is a poetry of dawn and spring, sunrise and blossom, of April and May, of mating birds, of opening buds and violets and primroses, of the pride of the eyes that quicken love and the other senses, so eloquently celebrated by Biron. It is a poetry that seems to expand, to dilate, under the pressure of some living force working from within, and each sonnet opens like a flower:

> From you have I been absent in the spring,
> When proud-pied April, dress'd in all his trim,
> Hath put a spirit of youth in every thing,
> That heavy Saturn laugh'd and leap'd with him.
> Yet nor the lays of birds, nor the sweet smell
> Of different flowers in odour and in hue,
> Could make me any summer's story tell,

Or from their proud lap pluck them where they grew:
Nor did I wonder at the lily's white,
Nor praise the deep vermilion in the rose;
They were but sweet, but figures of delight,
Drawn after you, you pattern of all those.
  Yet seem'd it winter still, and you away,
  As with your shadow I with these did play.

It is this princely poetry that flows over into the plays of this period, sometimes incongruously, and often undramatically, for such poetry is not the stuff out of which real men and women are created, nor is such unpredictable lyricism the medium in which action can be controlled. Thus Biron defends himself against the King of Navarre:

King. Biron is like an envious sneaping frost,
That bites the first-born infants of the spring.
  Biron. Well, say I am; why should proud summer boast,
Before the birds have any cause to sing?
Why should I joy in any abortive birth?
At Christmas I no more desire a rose
Than wish a snow in May's new-fangled shows.

When Benvolio wishes to tell Lady Montague that he has seen Romeo an hour before sunrise, he begins:

Madam, an hour before the worshipp'd sun
Peer'd forth the golden windows of the east.

Montague is well read in the *Sonnets*:

As is the bud bit with an envious worm,
Ere he can spread his sweet leaves to the air
Or dedicate his beauty to the sun.

The Poetry of Shakespeare's Plays

And the Capulets are even closer students of the sequence than the Montagues. Even Philip of France in *King John* knows number 33, and when he says:

> To solemnise this day the glorious sun
> Stays in his course and plays the alchemist,

the temptation is irresistible, and – or rather Shakespeare – adds:

> Turning with splendour of his precious eye
> The meagre cloddy earth to glittering gold.

Much of the verse spoken by Romeo and Juliet is pure lyric, bordering on the confines of music, love songs with so slender a dramatic significance that almost they might be abstracted from the play and applied to all young lovers whose tongues sound silver-sweet by night. Such verse makes little pretence to be dramatic, but sometimes verse that is intended to further the action forgets its function and slips into the same lyric vein. As a simple example, consider the difference between Othello's words when he silences the brawl in Cyprus and those of Escalus under similar circumstances. Othello says quite simply:

> Why, how now, ho! from whence ariseth this?
> Are we turn'd Turks, and to ourselves do that
> Which heaven hath forbid the Ottomites?
> For Christian shame, put by this barbarous brawl:
> He that stirs next to carve for his own rage
> Holds his soul light; he dies upon his motion.

The images compress the speech instead of extending it. Not so Escalus however:

> Rebellious subjects, enemies to peace,
> Profaners of this neighbour-stained steel –
> Will they not hear? What, ho! you men, you beasts,
> That quench the fire of your pernicious rage
> With purple fountains issuing from your veins,
> On pain of torture, from those bloody hands
> Throw your mistemper'd weapons to the ground,
> And hear the sentence of your moved prince.

Here the imagery leads to extension; the epithets and the long succession of stately phrases are decorative and not functional, and that Othello should call blood 'purple fountains issuing from your veins' is inconceivable.

The early histories are imperfectly dramatic because of their declamatory rhetoric, the lyrical plays because of their applied poetry; yet they have their rhetoric too. In *Richard II* there are pages of the threadbare but, still to the groundlings, apparently popular fustian of *Henry VI*, and as an example of undramatic poetry nothing could exceed the strange celebrations of the dying Melun in *King John*, V. iv, who, in a thirty-line speech of quibbling phrases and parenthetic clauses, runs with text-book precision through the whole gamut of rhetorical devices.

The pun is another element in the diffuseness of the lyrical plays, and in its extended form and outside merely farcical dialogue, first becomes prominent in the second scene of *The Two Gentlemen of Verona*, where Julia and Lucetta bandy musical terms, Lucetta returning the words with a characteristically delicate-indelicate twist. For the Shakespearean pun of this period is the main vehicle of Shakespearean bawdry; *Love's Labour's Lost* has a deal of this lightheartedly greasy quibbling, and the most lyrical of all the plays, *Romeo and Juliet*, is at the same time one of the most obscene. It will be found in a more passionate and concentrated form in Sonnets 135 and 136, the 'Will sonnets', and there is a similar concentration in *King John*, though with a difference. Here the wordplay is without unseemly innuendo, and is employed as a dramatic device to emphasize the grief of the distracted Constance; but in III. i, it degenerates into a competition between her and Pandulph as to who can, more or less intelligibly, repeat the same words with as many variations of meaning in the shortest possible compass, Constance pathetically emerging as a mere amateur after the papal legate's dazzling display of the wonders that can be worked with words in the trained and professional hands of a juggling Jesuit. Nowhere else in Shakespeare's plays is there an orgy on such a scale as this. Equally innocent, but more dramatic, is John of Gaunt's punning on his name in *Richard II*, II. i. Here the quibbling is associated more closely with the poetry:

> O, but they say the tongues of dying men
> Enforce attention like deep harmony...
> The setting sun, and music at the close,
> As the last taste of sweets, is sweetest last;

and with the splendid panegyric of England, 'this royal throne of kings'. Even more than metaphor the pun requires careful handling; neither will bear easily repetition and elaboration; the one may cool rapidly into conceit, the other into quibble, and whether conceit or quibble is justified, is successful, depends on the context; it is a question of circumstance and the degree of attenuation and abuse. The tragic heroes do not make the mistake of repeating and elaborating their puns, but the dying Gaunt's nice playing with his name is dramatically successful: the grief, and the grimness of image and jest, set against the unconcern of Richard and his favourites are, if not tragic, at least deeply moving. Then, twice at least in these plays Shakespeare anticipates the triumph of the tragic pun; in the prose of the mortally wounded Mercutio, 'Ask for me tomorrow, and you shall find me a grave man', and in the verse of Antonio, the merchant of Venice:

> For if the Jew do cut but deep enough,
> I'll pay it presently with all my heart.

Conceit, the conscious and fanciful pursuit of a resemblance, reaches its full distention in these plays, and is yet another cause of their prolixity. Thus the King of Navarre ingeniously compares his tears to coaches in which the Princess of France rides triumphing in his woes, and Lady Capulet describes Paris in terms of a book: his face the page on which delight is written with beauty's pen, his eyes the margin, and his binding a wife. This kind of writing, however beautiful, has little or nothing to do with the play, but in *Richard II* the conceits assume a different quality. Richard is a poet among princes, and though he talks almost entirely in conceits his poetry is dramatic, for it is characteristic, his self-pity finding a natural relief in labyrinthine thought and a search for tenuous affinities. Thus, when like glistening Phaethon he comes down from the walls of Flint Castle to surrender to Bolingbroke, he turns everything to favour and to prettiness by the lingering recital of his vanished glory, and by the new conceit started by the sight of Aumerle's tears, which deflect his thoughts into another channel as easily as those of a child:

> Aumerle, thou weep'st, my tender-hearted cousin!
> We'll make foul weather with despised tears,
> Our sighs and they shall lodge the summer corn...

The Poetry of Shakespeare's Plays

Richard needs no audience for his poetry any more than did the earlier historical characters for their declamation; in adversity he rarely talks to people, he talks to things, to the earth, to the crown, or rather he begins by talking to them, but when they have served their purpose of starting animage he forgets them in the complexities of the developing thought. Conceit leads naturally to quibble, and like Constance in *King John* he snatches at any word or phrase that offers opportunity for curious embellishment, though his elaboration is much more intellectual, less purely verbal than hers. Thus, how eagerly he seizes on Bolingbroke's 'The shadow of your sorrow hath destroy'd The shadow of your face', and when he is hammering out the conceit of his prison compared to the world, populating it with a generation of still-breeding thoughts, the discontented offspring of his soul and brain, how he welcomes the distraction of the music that suggests images that yet fresh images beget, until music, time, clock, bell and Bolingbroke are all swimming in his head in dreamlike confusion:

> I wasted time, and now doth time waste me;
> For now hath time made me his numbering clock:
> My thoughts are minutes; and with sighs they jar
> Their watches on unto mine eyes, the outward watch,
> Whereto my finger, like a dial's point,
> Is pointing still, in cleansing them from tears.
> Now sir, the sound that tells what hour it is
> Are clamorous groans, which strike upon my heart,
> Which is the bell...

Richard's habit of talking to things inevitably involves the pathetic fallacy, the investing of inanimate objects with human feelings; so when talking about himself – and he talks of little else – he employs the same device:

> For why, the senseless brands will sympathise
> The heavy accent of thy moving tongue,
> And in compassion weep the fire out;
> And some will mourn in ashes, some coal-black,
> For the deposing of a rightful king.

Such a conceit is as characteristic of parts of *King John* as it is of the essence of *Richard II*, and when Arthur pleads for his eyes he speaks perfect Richard:

> The iron of itself, though heat red-hot,
> Approaching near these eyes, would drink my tears
> And quench his fiery indignation...

Shakespeare rarely exploits the pathetic fallacy in his later plays, and even when he employs it in *Richard II* and *King John* he does so without sentimentality; it is as characteristic of Richard as is speaking thick of Hotspur, and is a legitimate and fitting mode of expression for the boy Arthur and the distracted Constance. Whatever the faults of Shakespeare, he cannot fairly be accused of sentimentality, of piling on the pathos to force a tear; on the contrary he may be, and sometimes is, accused of frigidity. 'He no sooner begins to move, than he counteracts himself,' wrote Jonson, 'and terror and pity, as they are rising in the mind, are checked and blasted by sudden frigidity.' Sir Walter Raleigh, too, finds that 'something of this chill mars the speeches of Arthur when he pleads with Hubert for his life'. But Arthur was not pleading for his life, he was pleading for his *eyes*, the loss of which for Shakespeare himself would have been the greatest of all calamities, and an appreciation of the inestimable value that he attached to the precious treasure of his sight adds to the pathos of Arthur's supplication:

The Poetry of Shakespeare's Plays

>Let me not hold my tongue, let me not, Hubert;
>Or, Hubert, if you will, cut out my tongue,
>So I may keep mine eyes: O, spare mine eyes.

In these plays, then, Shakespeare takes his time; if a word has more than one meaning or suggests another of similar sound he makes a pun or develops a quibble; if his imagination apprehends a relationship between things essentially dissimilar his fancy will not rest until it has discovered further points of congruity and has worked out a conceit, or if some detail of his theme – a rose, a sunrise, or a lady's eyes – fires his imagination, the play is forgotten until the lyrical impulse has had its way. And all, quibble, conceit, lyrical digression, and the dramatic nexus itself, the slender chain of events on which they are strung, are embellished with the graces and flourishes of poetry. Shakespeare himself in the person of Biron mockingly describes the style:

>Taffeta phrases, silken terms precise,
>   Three-piled hyperboles, spruce affectation,
>Figures pedantical; these summer-flies
>   Have blown me full of maggot ostentation.

This is truer of the first three plays of the series, particularly of *Love's Labour's Lost*, than of the remainder, but with some qualification and allowance for the element of caricature in the lines, it admirably fits the style of the greater part of all. Yet hyperbole, affectation, pedantry and ostentation do not necessarily preclude poetry; on the contrary, they are the very stuff out of which the poetry of this period is made. Especially the taffeta phrases, for this is pre-eminently the poetry of phrase, and the perfection of the single line within which the phrase is set. Sonnet 33, the octet of which is quoted above, is a succession of such lines, and if asked to describe this poetry of noun, adjective, and phrase, one might do worse than quote the line from the sestet, 'With all-triumphant splendour on my brow'.

Shakespeare, at this period, prefers the adverbial phrase to the adverb, 'with all-triumphant splendour' to 'triumphantly', and nearly always he employs the adjectival phrase in a similar manner. In one form it is even more characteristic than the adverbial phrase, for there is always an alternative mode of expression; thus we may say, and Shakespeare does in fact write, 'winter's ragged hand', but one can equally well say 'the ragged hand of winter', the image preceding the phrase which imaginatively it modifies, though grammatically modified by it. As the adverbial phrase is longer and more sonorous – more ostentatious, to use Biron's expression – than the adverb, so is the adjectival phrase for expressing the possessive case, and this is the form that Shakespeare prefers, the *Sonnets* being studded with these exquisitely turned and balanced lines:

Calls back the lovely April of her prime.
And stretched metre of an antique song.
Hung with the trophies of my lovers gone.
The rich-proud cost of outworn buried age.

Such lines are common in all six plays of the period:

Needs not the painted flourish of your praise.
On the white wonder of dear Juliet's hand.
To dwell in solemn shades of endless night.
Or in the beached margent of the sea.
Turning with splendour of his precious eye.
The shadow'd livery of the burnish'd sun.

The Poetry of Shakespeare's Plays

In passing, it is worth noting that the Bastard in King John parodies this style of writing:

> Drawn in the flattering table of her eye!
> Hang'd in the frowning wrinkle of her brow!
> And quarter'd in her heart!

All Shakespeare's nicest young men, the Bastard, Mercutio, Benedick, Hotspur, act as a sort of chorus, a link between Shakespeare and ourselves, humorous critics of his style lest it become too mannered and portentous. So Biron, the first of them, promises to forswear these taffeta phrases, though of course he does not, and fortunately Shakespeare himself, though fully alive to their dangers, was not yet willing to forswear them for a while.

As the lines are normally end-stopped, the main statement lies typically in the first half and the phrase in the second, the effect being to reduce the speed, to give weight and stateliness, and a ceremonious cadence to the line, an effect that is intensified by Shakespeare's partiality for polysyllabic concentrations. Sometimes the movement of the sonnet line is retarded by an accumulation of consonants between the vowels:

> The perfect ceremony of love's rite.

> Love's not Time's fool, though rosy lips and cheeks
> Within his bending sickle's compass come.

Sometimes by the use of the alliterative *w*:

> And do whate'er thou wilt, swift-footed Time,
> To the wide world and all her fading sweets.

Sonnets and Lyrical Plays

And often the initial speed is checked by the inversion of the first foot, a device which may, in conjunction with swelling *p*'s and *b*'s, give an effect of splendid pageantry and youthful pride, transforming an elegiac theme into something approaching the triumph of a paean:

Time doth transfix the flourish set on youth,
And delves the parallels in beauty's brow.

There is the same triumphant measure in the poetry of these plays:

Death, that hath suck'd the honey of thy breath,
Hath had no power yet upon thy beauty.

The line characteristic of the early comedies is based on a feminine ending, but as rhyme does not encourage the employment of a terminal redundant syllable, there is a modification in the sonnets and rhyming lyrical plays.[1] Here it is more formal, and based on the mid-line juxtaposition of trochaic words, generally a noun and its attendant epithet, as in, 'Needs not the *painted flourish* of your praise'. Once again, the effect is to reduce the speed of the line, partly because of the slight pause in the middle of the central foot, but mainly because of the reversed rhythm suggested by this formal disposition of natural trochees, a rhythm that is sometimes emphasized by assonance, as in,

O, how shall summer's honey breath hold out?'[2]

This is an early and elementary form of the linking of assonance to rhythm, the effect being confined to the line. Another is the simple sequence of trochaic words assonantally related, as in Sonnet 106, 'When in the chronicle of wasted time', with its series, *wasted, making, ladies, blazon, praises*; and a similar effect is achieved by repeating the same words (*beauty* is nearly always repeated), as in Sonnet 18, 'Shall I compare thee to a summer's day?' *sometime* being twice repeated, and *summer* three times. But in these early sequences the relation between assonance and rhythm is only slight, owing to the wide distribution of the words and lack of subordinate links, and the extended assonance of this lyrical poetry is primarily a means of harmonizing and integrating a passage. This again can most easily be illustrated from the *Sonnets*, and number 12, 'When I do count the clock', is a particularly beautiful example. In the first quatrain the emphasis is on *a* and *i*: 'brave day', 'hideous night'; in the second on the long *e* of 'trees', 'leaves', 'heat', 'green', 'sheaves', 'bier', 'beard'; then in the final quatrain all these vowels are woven about the deep *u*'s of 'beauty do' and 'beauties do',

> Then of thy beauty do I question make,
> That thou among the wastes of time must go,
> Since sweets and beauties do themselves forsake
> And die as fast as they see others grow;

and the poem culminates in the counterpoint of the couplet,

> And nothing 'gainst Time's scythe can make defence
> Save breed, to brave him when he takes thee hence.

But alliteration is more characteristic, or at least a more prominent characteristic, of the early poetry than assonance, and how by the time of the sonnets and lyrical plays Shakespeare had transformed the crude repetition of the early histories into something very like music may be judged by comparing this from 2 *Henry VI*,

> The sons of York, thy betters in their birth,
> Shall be their father's bail; and bane to those
> That for my surety will refuse the boys!

with this from Sonnet 2,

> When forty winters shall besiege thy brow
> And dig deep trenches in thy beauty's field,
> Thy youth's proud livery, so gazed on now,
> Will be a tatter'd weed, of small worth held;[3]

and with this from *Richard II*,

> The bay-trees in our country are all wither'd,
> And meteors fright the fixed stars of heaven;
> The pale-faced moon looks bloody on the earth,
> And lean-look'd prophets whisper fearful change.[4]

As the vowel demands to be repeated and perpetually varied throughout any passage of prose or verse, so does the consonant. In the first, the initial *b*'s are simply a part of the rhetoric, but in the next two they are varied with the kindred sounds of *p, f, v, w, m*, and are of the essence of the poetry. These were always favourite letters with Shakespeare, but the alliterative use of the labials is as characteristic of the poetry of this period as is the phrase, the splendour of which is so often dependent upon it. Romeo's last speech beginning,

> For here lies Juliet, and her beauty makes
> This vault a feasting presence full of light,

is the perfection of this alliterative poetry. Though Shakespeare was thinking primarily of his subject matter and the sonnet form when he wrote Sonnet 76, it may be that he also glanced at his style, of which it is so excellent a pattern:

> Why is my verse so barren of new pride,
> So far from variation or quick change?
> Why with the time do I not glance aside
> To new-found methods and to compounds strange?
> Why write I still all one, ever the same,
> And keep invention in a noted weed,
> That every word doth almost tell my name,
> Showing their birth and where they did proceed?

Sometimes Shakespeare's contemporaries achieve a comparable music in their sonnets, notably Daniel and Drayton, but they do not as consistently produce his perfection of phrase and line, his pervasive harmony of consonant and vowel, and in no other dramatist is there anything comparable.

Such a form of drama, half play, half poem, or rather a sequence of poems on a tragic or comic theme, in which the phrase, the line, and the lyrical episode are so important, might easily have disintegrated into something too unshapely or amorphous for the stage. Yet perhaps no other plays leave one with such a vivid impression of unity as the first four of this group, and this, paradoxically enough, because of the lyric form itself, for of all poetry the lyric is the most pure in origin and single in its statement. They seem, as Pater remarks, to have evolved from a song or ballad lying at their roots, 'all the various expression of the conflict of character and circumstance falling at last into the compass of a single melody, or musical theme'. Of *Romeo and Juliet*, one feels, is this particularly true, a play in which the related lyric utterance of the sonnet, aubade, epithalamium and elegy are the interwoven music of a symphony. It is the organic form of romantic art described by Coleridge, innate, and shaping 'as it develops itself from within', and not to be confused with a preconceived form imposed by extraneous forces, by the calculated application of the unities of neo-classical theorists.

This imaginative unity is intensified in other ways. Every Shakespearean play has its peculiar atmosphere, every tragedy its peculiar imagery, and there can be few readers of *Romeo and Juliet* who are not left with the impression of prevailing darkness pierced by brilliant light. There is nothing sinister in this darkness, which is that of a velvety summer night, nor is there anything of evil either in the characters or in the environment;[5] the darkness suggests quite simply death and the blindness of chance, and light the conflict of youth and beauty with these two powers. The impression of darkness is induced in the first place by making all the most important scenes take place at night; of the five in which Romeo and Juliet appear together, only one, the insignificant II. vi, is by daylight, and even that is in Friar Laurence's cell. But in addition to this, the play is full of references to, and images drawn from night, reaching a climax in Juliet's great invocation, 'Come, night, come, Romeo', in which Romeo is addressed as day in night, light in darkness, and night becomes the symbol both of love and death, the other word and image that runs through the play intensifying the atmosphere of darkness. The conflicting element of light is suggested by the lyrical descriptions of sunrise, and sometimes the darkness is scattered by the flare of torches, at others pierced by the thin fixed points of the stars. But the dominant word and image, as in *Love's Labour's Lost*, is the eye, the source of light, and all these words, *night, death, eyes, stars, torches*, run like threads through the play, weaving a shadowy pattern, dark and bright, a pattern that is finally restated and perfected by Romeo in his last speech.

In *A Midsummer Night's Dream* there is the same imaginative fusion of events. Even rarer than Puck, the fairy link between the four groups of characters, there are the dreams. All the lovers dream; Titania has a vision of an ass, and the ass himself a most rare vision of a queen; Hippolyta begins the play with a dream image, and Puck rounds off all – shadows, visions and dreams – with his lovely apologetic octosyllabics, 'Think this weak and idle theme, No more yielding but a dream'. But there is an element even more pervasive than dreams, almost, it might be said, a character more ubiquitous than Puck. This is the moon, whose light suffuses all the characters irrespective of rank or origin, heroes, lovers, clowns and fairies, subduing everything to the insubstantial silver of a vision, and intensifying the dreamlike quality of the play. The moon is either referred to quite simply, or personified as the goddess of chastity, or more obliquely evoked as an image, and in the comic plot the very earthy and pedantic artisans wrest her from her sphere, unsex her, and 'disfigure' her upon the stage as a lantern in the hand of the tailor Starveling. And when Puck in his epilogue in the great hall draws all together, we know that the towers and turrets of the palace are still silvered, for 'the wolf behowls the moon'.

The imagery of *King John* is unique because of the frequency with which it takes the form of personification, either direct or implied. Of direct personification that of Death is the commonest; Prince Henry sees it as the besieger of the outworks of the body, and then of the final citadel of the mind; for the Bastard it is a steel-jawed monster 'mousing the flesh of men', but it is also, as for Constance, a rotten carcass, a putrescent corpse. The extraordinary amount of indirect or implied personification may be illustrated by taking that in a short scene; thus in the seventy lines of III. iii the fat ribs of peace must be fed upon, John's soul counts Hubert her creditor, Hubert's oath lives in John's bosom, time creeps, the proud day is watchful and all too wanton to give John audience, the midnight bell's iron tongue and brazen mouth sound on into the drowsy ear of night, melancholy bakes, blood runs and tickles, and laughter is an idiot. The river image is more insistent in *King John* than in any other play, and yet it is the fire image, coupled sometimes with that of a burning fever, that is the predominant one and much the most dramatically significant; blood is set on fire, eyes are red as fire, and bullets wrapped in fire make a shaking fever in the walls; John is burned up with wrath, Philip hopes that he will turn to ashes, and in his dying speech John recapitulates and harmonizes the imagery:

> Ay, marry, now my soul hath elbow-room;
> It would not out at windows nor at doors.
> There is so hot a summer in my bosom,
> That all my bowels crumble up to dust:
> I am a scribbled form, drawn with a pen
> Upon a parchment, and against this fire
> Do I shrink up...
> And none of you will bid the winter come
> To thrust his icy fingers in my maw,
> Nor let my kingdom's rivers take their course
> Through my burn'd bosom, nor entreat the north
> To make his bleak winds kiss my parched lips
> And comfort me with cold. I do not ask you much,
> I beg cold comfort...
> The tackle of my heart is crack'd and burn'd,
> And all the shrouds wherewith my life should sail
> Are turned to one thread, one little hair:

The Poetry of Shakespeare's Plays

> My heart hath one poor string to stay it by,
> Which holds but till thy news be uttered;
> And then all this thou seest is but a clod
> And module of confounded royalty.

No praise could be too high for the writing of this, and perhaps no other passage in any of the plays has quite the same intense visual quality. Every line, almost every word, is a picture, for in addition to the fire, river and ship images there is the personification implied in elbow, fingers, kiss, hair, reinforced by the enumeration of other parts of the body. Then there are the characteristic grim and tragic puns, the shrivelling *r*'s, and the brilliant assonantal opposition of the *u*'s and *i*'s that symbolize the conflicting forces of heat and cold: *summer, bosom, crumble, dust; winter, icy fingers, kingdom's rivers*. Nothing in John's life became him like the leaving it; without his poetry he would be what Hazlitt called him, a cowardly and contemptible character that excites disgust and loathing; with it he approaches the stature of a tragic hero.

King John is not altogether at ease in its position as one of the last of the lyrical plays; it has characteristics that suggest both an earlier and later date, and less than we should expect of the naturalism that gradually invades the verse. The earliest traces of this are to be found in humorous or semi-humorous soliloquy, and in the narrative and descriptive passages that Shakespeare always took such delight in writing: in Richard III's sardonic and jocular asides, in Petruchio's wooing of Kate and Gremio's account of their marriage, in Biron's soliloquy on love. But the first extensive and most memorable passage of this new naturalism is the interlude of Mercutio's Queen Mab speech, which stands out from its context as clearly as the Player's speech in *Hamlet*. Here Mercutio is swept away on the wings of his imagination, which fly straight on impatient of rhetorical flourish and lyrical display, so that the passage runs at a speed that at once distinguishes it from its context. Then, there is a great catholicity of diction. Shakespeare never developed a restricted and exclusive poetic diction as did Milton and the Augustans, a diction, in the words of Dryden, 'at once refined from the grossness of domestic use and free from the harshness of terms appropriate to particular arts'; his progress was, indeed, just the reverse of this, an escape from a conventional Elizabethan diction which, though it did not reject the harshness of terms appropriate to particular arts, preferred the obviously 'poetic' word to that unrefined from the grossness of domestic use. He was always prepared to accept the homely image as well as the homely word; nevertheless, the proportion of 'poetical' images, phrases, periphrases and words becomes smaller as his work becomes more dramatic; or, to put it the other way round, his work becomes more dramatic because the verse becomes less obviously poetical; which in turn is only another way of saying that the tempo of his verse quickens.

> This is that very Mab
> That plats the manes of horses in the night,
> And bakes the elf-locks in foul sluttish hairs,
> Which once untangled much misfortune bodes.

There is scarcely a 'poetical' word or phrase in the whole speech; and the verse *moves*. Compare this with the quibbling that precedes it:

> I am too sore enpierced with his shaft
> To soar with his light feathers, and so bound,
> I cannot bound a pitch above dull woe.

The Poetry of Shakespeare's Plays

This is an eddy without progression. And when Mercutio is arrested in the torrent of his tale he returns to the dilated lyricism that loses itself in a succession of phrases and relative clauses:

> True, I talk of dreams;
> Which are the children of an idle brain,
> Begot of nothing but vain fantasy,
> Which is as thin of substance as the air,
> And more inconstant than the wind, who woos
> Even now the frozen bosom of the north...

But, as Benvolio says, 'the date is out of such prolixity' – or almost so. For, in addition to the Queen Mab interlude, there are other indications of a quickening tempo even in *Romeo and Juliet*. Sometimes it is merely a compression of phrase, *bent of love, respective lenity*, but sometimes Juliet, the most direct speaker of them all, weaves closer the texture of a whole passage:

> Therefore, out of thy long-experienced time,
> Give me some present counsel; or, behold,
> 'Twixt my extremes and me this bloody knife
> Shall play the umpire, arbitrating that
> Which the commission of thy years and art
> Could to no issue of true honour bring.

Such writing has more in common with the later plays than with the *Sonnets*, and after *Romeo and Juliet* never again is heard, or rather seen, in all its splendour 'the proud full sail of his great verse', as Shakespeare describes that of his rival, and so exactly describes his own at this period; the labials driving the stately vessel of the phrase slowly along the line; the line so often self-contained, balanced, and graced with all the pageantry of rhetoric; the tackle of the verse straining under the pressure of the quibbles, conceits and compound epithets: earth-treading stars and lazy-pacing clouds.

Even in *A Midsummer Night's Dream* there is a different tone, though not in the language of the lovers, which is curiously archaic, literary and conventional. The fairies are much more direct and natural, perhaps because they act with a mischievous singleness of purpose impossible to their bewitched and bewildered victims. Like the lovers, generally they speak in rhyme, sometimes in delicate octosyllabics, more often in decasyllabics, but lovely as their rhyming poetry is, it is surpassed by the hundred lines of blank verse in which Oberon quarrels with Titania. Here Shakespeare, the lyric poet, is in his element; character is irrelevant; let Oberon be unreasonable and Titania querulous; the theme, a quarrel about what you will, and he is free to write about the floods in Warwickshire. It is Titania who speaks the poetry. She begins in conventional bucolic vein, but stung by Oberon's taunts she turns on him:

> These are the forgeries of jealousy;
> And never, since the middle summer's spring,
> Met we on hill, in dale, forest, or mead,
> By paved fountain or by rushy brook,
> Or in the beached margent of the sea,
> But with thy brawls thou hast disturbed our sport.

This is the poetry of the *Sonnets*, with its self-contained lines and related verbal trochees, its beautiful mutation of consonants and its phrases – yet it is the sonnet poetry with a difference; the old ceremonious modes of expression are giving place to a language that approximates more closely to that really spoken by men, as well as by fairies, and the formality of the sophisticated line is modified by a more natural rhythm. There follows the unforgettable picture of the English countryside heavy with the rains of a wet summer: the straining ox, the sweating ploughman, the unripened corn, the empty fold in the flooded field, the fat crows, lean sheep, and the mud in the nine men's morris, the realism of which forms a delightful contrast to the more artificial style of the remainder: the conceit of the moon pale with anger, and the quiet perfection of,

> hoary-headed frosts
> Fall in the fresh lap of the crimson rose;
> And on old Hiems' thin and icy crown
> An odorous chaplet of sweet summer buds
> Is, as in mockery set.

Titania continues,

> His mother was a votaress of my order:
> And, in the spiced Indian air, by night,
> Full often hath she gossip'd by my side;
> And sat with me on Neptune's yellow sands,
> Marking the embarked traders on the flood;
> When we have laugh'd to see the sails conceive
> And grow big-bellied with the wanton wind;
> Which she, with pretty and with swimming gait
> Following, – her womb then rich with my young squire, –
> Would imitate, and sail upon the land,
> To fetch me trifles, and return again,
> As from a voyage, rich with merchandise.

Though this too is dependent for its beauty largely on the quality of its phrases, it is by no means entirely so. Assonance is beginning to compete in importance with alliteration: *yellow – follow, fetch – rich – merchant, swimming gait – imitate*; there is the internal rhyme of *mark – bark* in the line that might come from *The Merchant of Venice*, and above all there is the felicitous rhythm of the overflowing line, 'with pretty and with swimming gait Following', something very different from the stubborn dialogue of the lovers. It is not only that the restrictive unit of the line is being broken by the overflows and mid-line pauses; a new rhythm is imposed by the pauses in mid-foot, by the real reversal in the dactylic *following*, and by the apparent reversal in *trifles* and *voyage*. The lyric line is extended, and moves to a more varied measure. It is not dramatic poetry, but it is narrative poetry such as had never before been heard in English. There is a similar movement in the blank verse of Theseus and Hippolyta, in the magnificent, though dramatically quite irrelevant description of the hunt, where the vowels, like the voices of the hounds, are so artfully matched like bells. It is the blank verse, the poetry of *The Merchant of Venice*.

This more natural diction and more seeming-natural rhythm are accompanied by a parallel development of the imagery, well illustrated in *A Midsummer Night's Dream*. Thus, the lovers, on whom Shakespeare seems deliberately to have fastened his half-outmoded manner, speak the old emblematic language; Helena's eyes are crystal, her lips kissing cherries, her hands whiter than 'high Taurus' snow, Fann'd with the eastern wind'. Beautiful as are such variations, these stock literary images are ceasing to attract attention, and the bird image in which the unromantic Puck so vigorously describes the flight of the rude mechanicals is something very different:

The Poetry of Shakespeare's Plays

> As wild geese that the creeping fowler eye,
> Or russet-pated choughs, many in sort,
> Rising and cawing at the gun's report,
> Sever themselves and madly sweep the sky,
> So, at his sight, away his fellows fly.

Clearly, this picture is spontaneous, the half-forgotten memories of these sights and sounds observed in the fields about Stratford leaping into full consciousness as the perfect equivalent for the scattering and shrieking Athenians. There are, of course, similar observed images in the earlier plays, and in *Titus Andronicus* is a companion, though less particularized, picture,

> You sad-faced men, people and sons of Rome,
> By uproars sever'd, as a flight of fowl
> Scatter'd by winds and high tempestuous gusts;

but in these later lyrical plays the original and observed image is becoming much more frequent.

Puck's image, however, is still narrative in form, too lengthily developed to be dramatic, and as a contrast to the deliberate unfolding of this single simile, consider Salisbury's protest against King John's second coronation:

> In this the antique and well noted face
> Of plain old form is much disfigured;
> And, like a shifted wind unto a sail,
> It makes the course of thoughts to fetch about,
> Startles and frights consideration,
> Makes sound opinion sick and truth suspected,
> For putting on so new a fashion'd robe.

SONNETS AND LYRICAL PLAYS

In these seven lines there are as many images, all but one metaphors, each rapidly materializing, and dissolving into its successor before it can be fully apprehended, so that the apparent discord of the sequence – face, wind, ship, consideration startled, opinion sick, truth a suspect, robe – is resolved by the speed itself into a composite image of the confusion caused by hurly-burly innovation, in much the same way as the hues of a colour circle are harmonized by its revolution. This is the beginning of the more complex and dramatic imagery of the later style, a further development of which takes place in *The Merchant of Venice*.

Few plays of Shakespeare are better known, and in this sense more popular, than *The Merchant of Venice*, and it is unfortunate, therefore, that apart from its poetry it is one of the least pleasant. Admittedly the scene and fable have a superficial charm; there are all the elements that go to make a romantic comedy: Venice in the shimmering and disintegrating light of day, the giddy traffic of the Rialto, the argosies with portly sail; Venice flickering in the torchlight of masquers and revellers; the moonlight sleeping upon Belmont; and flitting about the alleys and canals and country houses the brilliantly dressed and gaily chattering figures of Renaissance Italy. And yet it is all so empty, so heartless; the voices ring thinly and the laughter awakes no echo. Apart from Shylock there is no character who feels deeply; Antonio is only a lay figure about whom revolve the action and a crew of adventurers whose main business is to make easy profits out of matrimony, and whose pastime is Jew-baiting. Nor are the ladies much more attractive; there is a touch of priggishness and hypocrisy about Portia, and Jessica, whatever else she may be, is a renegade and a thief.

Yet the play contains some of the loveliest poetry that Shakespeare ever wrote, and is of exceptional interest and importance. It is the last of the great series of lyrical dramas, and at the same time the first of the sequence of comedies in which prose is as important a medium as verse. It is a transitional play, the link between Shakespeare the lyric poet and Shakespeare the dramatic poet, the play in which is heard almost for the last time the pure poetry of the early period, and in which for the first time a major character speaks serious prose.

The scene opens with Antonio's wondering why he is so sad, and in a slow-moving lyrical passage that reads like a duet in music his friends suggest that it is on account of the ventures that he has at sea:

> I should not see the sandy hour-glass run,
> But I should think of shallows and of flats,
> And see my wealthy Andrew dock'd in sand
> Vailing her high top lower than her ribs
> To kiss her burial. Should I go to church
> And see the holy edifice of stone,
> And not bethink me straight of dangerous rocks,
> Which touching but my gentle vessel's side
> Would scatter all her spices on the stream,
> Enrobe the roaring waters with my silks?

None of the plays has a lovelier opening than this; it is the language of Titania,

> And sat with me on Neptune's yellow sands,
> Marking the embarked traders on the flood,

the blank verse of *A Midsummer Night's Dream*, in which the rhythm is beginning to overlap the lines, and assonance to assume the importance of alliteration. In no other play are assonance, as a purely harmonic device, and internal rhyme (sometimes merely the repetition of the same word) so highly developed as in *The Merchant of Venice*. In Salarino's speech, for example, there is *sandy, and, sand, Andrew, shallow*; *gentle vessel*; *roaring waters*; *dock, rock*; *kiss, this*; *sea* and the threefold *see*. Then in his next speech we can clearly detect the beginning of the rhythm in which an imposed reversed beat is emphasized by assonance and extended beyond the line:

> Now, by two-*headed Janus*,
> *Nature* hath *framed strange fellows* in her time...
> Though *Nestor* swear the *jest be* laughable.

The true trochee of *nature* is linked by assonance to the 'false' one of *Janus*, to which is attached *headed*, which in turn is related to *fellows*, *Nestor* and *jest be*. The construction is similar to Viola's,

> 'Tis *beauty truly* blent, whose red and white
> *Nature's* own sweet and cunning hand *laid on*:
> Lady...

In I. iii Shylock recounts in prose what Salarino and Salanio have already said in verse, but when Antonio enters the language rises again to the greater dignity of verse. Dramatically, the verse in this and the other Shylock scenes is an advance on anything that Shakespeare had yet written; Shylock *talks* to the other characters, and forces them to talk to him instead of addressing the audience, and the language is more natural, more functional, a medium for the development of character and action; it advances more steadily, with fewer excursions into pure poetry, and more easily, without the encumbrance of a formal rhetoric. Yet this gain in ease and dramatic quality is achieved not without some sacrifice of the poetry. Much of the most

The Poetry of Shakespeare's Plays

memorable poetry of the early plays is in the digressions and elaborations, the personal, lyrical, and scarcely dramatic utterances of Shakespeare himself, when for the moment he abandons the action, and in the person of one of the characters, major or minor, pleasant or unpleasant, pursues a theme that powerfully moves him; when, for example, Biron speaks so eloquently of lovers' eyes, and Proteus of music, the poetry takes control, and the characters are little more than a pretext for the expression of Shakespeare's own feelings. In the Shylock scenes, however, he imposes on himself a severer discipline and rarely intervenes in order to speak himself. As a result the writing, though more dramatic, is less 'poetical', for he had not yet developed the compound metaphor and embracing rhythm which, in the later plays, take the place of simple image and decorative line, and this throws into strong relief the undramatic and rhetorical poetry of which so much of the remainder of the play is composed.

There are, however, lines indicative of the compressed poetry that was to come, as when Morocco in II. vii, after a passage of spectacular Marlovian rhetoric, rejects the leaden casket with the words,

> it were too gross
> To rib her cerecloth in the obscure grave.

Then the second casket scene is almost an epitome of Shakespearean characteristics, both of the early and middle styles, and admirably illustrates the transitional nature of the play. Arragon advances to the front of the stage and declaims to the audience in the moralizing and exclamatory rhetoric of the early histories, though with a very different rhythm, then, although he retains the rhetorical structure, the texture of the verse is suddenly tautened, and prolixity becomes a concentration of metaphor more complex than that of Salisbury's:

> How much low peasantry would then be glean'd
> From the true seed of honour! and how much honour
> Pick'd from the chaff and ruin of the times,
> To be new-varnish'd!

Glean, seed, chaff, ruin, varnish; and how the double image of chaff and ruin, the particular and the general, intensifies the brilliance of the illumination. He uses a similar construction when he compares the 'fool multitude' to the martlet, which

> Builds in the weather on the outward wall,
> Even in the force and road of casualty.

Though the martlet simile is Shakespearean of any period, the compound metaphor of the last line, like 'chaff and ruin of the times', is one of the first of those that become a major characteristic of the middle style. A few lines later a servant announces Bassanio's approach in verse that might have come out of a sonnet:

> A day in April never came so sweet,
> To show how costly summer was at hand.

The first scene of the third act is memorable as the first great prose scene in Shakespeare, that is, the first in which a major character speaks nothing but serious dramatic prose. It seems probable that Shakespeare originally conceived Shylock merely as a figure of fun to be baited to make a Christian holiday, but if so he had abandoned the conception when he wrote this scene. It opens quietly with

The Poetry of Shakespeare's Plays

Salanio and Salarino talking of, even jesting at, Antonio's losses, but when Shylock comes in they turn quite naturally to the more congenial sport of Jew-baiting. Then Shylock begins to speak – in prose that has the balance and repetition of the Psalms, and like the Psalms a rhythm that still approaches but continually eludes the regularity of verse: 'I would my daughter were dead at my foot, and the jewels in her ear. Would she were hearsed at my foot, and the ducats in her coffin.'

After such grief and hate, the lovemaking of Portia and Bassanio sounds almost shallow and impertinent, and yet there is exquisite poetry when Portia calls for music – music that must always be associated with *The Merchant of Venice*:

> Let music sound while he doth make his choice;
> Then, if he lose, he makes a swan-like end,
> Fading in music...

The variation of *Let music* in *Then, if he lose*, and the elegiac echo and reversal of *music – make his* in *Fading in music*, a much favoured cadence in the poetry of a few years later, are unforgettable. One would have expected Bassanio to make straight for the golden casket, but he rejects it, quibbling and moralizing on meretricious beauty in the manner of Sonnet 68:

> Thus ornament is but the guiled shore
> To a most dangerous sea; the beauteous scarf
> Veiling an Indian beauty,

and it is worth noting how Shakespeare at this period associated certain sounds and images: the sea, India, costly textiles, and the syllable *ar*, as in 'Enrobe the roaring waters with my silks', 'The scarfed bark puts from her native bay', 'spiced Indian air...embarked traders on the flood...rich with merchandise'.

The court scene is the most consistently dramatic that Shakespeare had yet written; that is, the first big scene in which he applies all his genius to the conduct of the action, never neglecting it to pursue a digression however attractive, never subordinating it to the language, never – or never for more than a moment – allowing the poetry to take control. But aesthetically it is inferior to the rest of the play, partly for this very reason, partly because the theme is so repugnant and the characters so unlovable. Shakespeare's genius was as yet incompletely articulated: the poet is still in advance of the dramatist, and here Shakespeare is primarily a dramatist. Portia's central speech on Mercy finds its way into most anthologies, for this platitudinous moralizing in inferior verse has long been one of the popularly accepted standards of Shakespeare's poetry. It is, as Hazlitt observes, 'very well – but there are a thousand finer ones in Shakespeare'. Of course there are, and a century of them in *The Merchant of Venice*.

The play is over; the dramatist has finished, but there still remains a trifling matter of a couple of rings to serve as pretext for another scene, a scene that can be all music and poetry and moonlight in the manner of *A Midsummer Night's Dream*. The place can be the garden of Portia's house at Belmont, the broken Jew can be forgotten and left to hang himself in Venice, and for characters there are three pairs of young lovers. After a scene of pure drama Shakespeare can afford to write a scene of pure poetry – though, as it happens, it is for the last time. And so the stage is set for the beautiful and bawdy nonsense of the rings.

The Poetry of Shakespeare's Plays

> The moon shines bright: in such a night as this,
> When the sweet wind did gently kiss the trees
> And they did make no noise, in such a night
> Troilus methinks mounted the Troyan walls,
> And sighed his soul toward the Grecian tents,
> Where Cressid lay that night.

The harmony of internal rhyme and assonance throughout this wonderful duet of Lorenzo and Jessica almost makes a formal rhyme-scene appear a clumsy and mechanical contrivance. News is brought that Portia is at hand, but Lorenzo decides to stay and welcome her in the garden. He calls for music, though what he speaks himself is almost music:

> How *sweet* the moon*light sleeps* upon this bank!
> *Here will* we *sit*, and *let* the sounds of *music*
> *Creep* in our *ears*: soft *still*ness and the *night*
> Become the *touches* of *sweet harmony*.
> *Sit, Jessica. Look* how the floor of heaven
> *Is thick inlaid* with patines of *bright gold*:
> There's not the *smallest orb* which thou be*hold*'st
> But in his motion *like* an angel sings,
> *Still* quiring to the young-eyed cherubins;
> *Such harmony* is in *immortal souls*:
> But whilst this muddy *vesture* of *decay*
> *Doth grossly close* it in, we cannot *hear* it.

Portia enters unobserved, and the poetry shifts to her, though it lacks something of the unalloyed purity of Lorenzo's; there is a slight touch of her affectation and pedantry. She stops the music, and the magic is over.

As a play *The Merchant of Venice* is both made and marred by Shylock; he is himself one of the triumphs of

SONNETS AND LYRICAL PLAYS

Shakespeare's dramatic genius, and at the same time a main cause of its sudden development; he taught Shakespeare a dramatic language. On the other hand, simply because he is what he is, he lays bare the baser qualities of the other characters, the selfishness, insincerity, brutality, that are only skinned and filmed by their virtues. It is a mercy that Benedick and Beatrice, Rosalind and Viola were not exposed to his influence. But as poetry the play is beyond reproach. Shakespeare rarely surpassed this poetry in which the lyric line of the *Sonnets* is wedded to the more liberal movement of the verse of the next period.

1. The proportion of feminine to masculine endings in the first five lyrical plays is only half that in the early comedies. *The Merchant of Venice* returns to the same proportion as *The Two Gentlement of Verona*.
2. As in so many other ways, Keats comes nearest to Shakespeare in this quality of line and phrase:
   And be among her cloudy trophies hung.
   Rich in the simple worship of a day.
3. The slow and solemn measure of these lines is worth remarking, the flow of the verse being checked by the obstruction of the heavy triple stresses, *dig deep trenches, youth's proud livery, small worth held*.
4. Compare KEATS, *Psyche*: No heat of pale mouth'd prophet dreaming; and *Timon*, IV. iii: Nor sight of priests in holy vestments bleeding.
5. *Romeo and Juliet* is remarkable in being an Elizabethan tragedy not only without a villain, but without a single unpleasant character; disaster is brought about by circumstance or fate, so that it might almost be called 'The Tragedy of Errors'. After Aaron in *Titus Andronicus*, the next real villain is Claudius in *Hamlet*, and it is the concentration of evil in the tragedies that follow that so distinguishes them. *Antony and Cleopatra* is almost as free from evil as *Romeo and Juliet*.

Part Four

HISTORICAL AND ROMANTIC COMEDIES

1 Henry IV, *2 Henry IV*, *Henry V*,
The Merry Wives of Windsor, *Much Ado about Nothing*,
As You Like It, *Twelfth Night*.

As the early plays are remarkable for their high proportion of blank verse, and the lyrical plays for their rhyme, so the comedies of this group are remarkable for their preponderance of prose. Of the 28,000 lines of prose that Shakespeare wrote, nearly half are contained in these seven plays, in which the ratio of prose to verse is nearly two to one, whereas in those preceding them it is only about one to seven. Shakespeare had always used prose for low comedy, indeed it might be said that he had confined it to low comedy, and as in the six early histories there is scarcely any comedy at all it follows that there is scarcely any prose. There is comedy enough in the other early plays, but the prose is spoken by the humbler characters, the greater dignity of verse being reserved for the heroes and heroines. The middle histories differ from the early ones in having uproarious sub-plots, dominated by the prose-speaking Falstaff, but this does not account entirely for the prose; in these plays, histories and romantic comedies alike, Shakespeare takes the momentous step of extending its use to the main characters: thus Rosalind and Orlando make love in prose, Benedick and Beatrice scarcely speak anything else, and that inveterate talker Prince Henry speaks the same language as Falstaff, and even when king argues with his soldiers and woos his bride in prose.

After writing *The Merchant of Venice* and creating, almost as a by-product, his first great character in comedy and the first main character to speak serious prose, it may be that Shakespeare realized that the date of his former prolixity was out, and that if he was going to create character he must eschew lyrical dialogue and resist the blandishments of those themes that always moved him to pure poetry. Or it may be that he was stimulated by the appearance of a rival in the person of Ben Jonson, whose first comedy, *The Case is Altered*, a mixture of prose and verse, was probably written in 1597, and whose Prologue to *Every Man in his Humour* (1598) is partly a criticism of the contemporary drama, and partly a claim that his plays are those of

> deeds, and language, such as men do use,
> And persons, such as comedy would choose,
> When she would show an image of the times.

Whatever the reason, the language of these next plays is a much closer approximation to that really spoken by men; rhyming dialogue almost disappears, lyric is virtually confined to the songs, prose becomes the staple medium, the blank verse itself is chastened, and in place of the artificial lyrical drama there emerges the comedy of character, of Falstaff and Prince Henry, Benedick and Beatrice, Rosalind and Jaques, Viola and Malvolio – but then *Twelfth Night* has a quality beyond that of the others.

Prose does not to the same extent as verse invite the lyrical excursus and over-elaboration of detail, and from its discipline and restraint Shakespeare learned to write dramatic verse, verse that is geared more closely to the action and rarely deviates from the matter in hand, but moves forthright with a steady, at times with an almost inexorably steady, pace, for in the histories he sometimes found compensation for lyric utterance in the overextended oratory of his spiritual and temporal princes.

A good example of this style is Henry IV's rebuke to the Prince of Wales (1 *Henry IV*, III. ii):

Historical and Romantic Comedies

> I know not whether God will have it so,
> For some displeasing service I have done,
> That, in his secret doom, out of my blood
> He'll breed revengement and a scourge for me;
> But thou dost in thy passages of life
> Make me believe that thou art only mark'd
> For the hot vengeance and the rod of heaven
> To punish my mistreadings. Tell me else,
> Could such inordinate and low desires,
> Such poor, such bare, such lewd, such mean attempts,
> Such barren pleasures, rude society,
> As thou art match'd withal and grafted to,
> Accompany the greatness of thy blood,
> And hold their level with thy princely heart?

It could scarcely be more straightforward than that; diction and syntax are simple and natural, and there are no declamatory tumidities and elliptical constructions to impede the verse that flows with a stately and even movement from beginning to end. Its great virtue is its clarity, but it has lost the brilliance of phrase and line of the early poetry and not yet acquired the elasticity and interpenetrating rhythm of the later. The imagery is interesting: a series of metaphors, unobtrusive and evenly distributed in accordance with the open texture of the verse, all of them very simple, and merely restatements in precise and concrete terms of the abstract qualities to which they are linked: 'revengement and a scourge', 'vengeance and the rod', 'match'd and grafted'. This linking of words, phrases and clauses by means of the conjunction 'and' is perhaps the most obvious characteristic of this middle style, a parallelism that contributes to the spaciousness of the verse, and gives to the long Lancastrian recitatives a pronounced epic flavour.

The Poetry of Shakespeare's Plays

Shakespeare's writing of prose dialogue was, no doubt, the main cause of this greater simplicity of diction and imagery, as also of the greater naturalness of the verse as a whole, prose rhythms and colloquial constructions encouraging the breaking down of the restrictive verse line, particularly by a variation of the length of the rhetorical unit and the position of the mid-line pauses. As dialogue is beginning to coincide more closely with the action, so is it beginning to coincide with character as well. There is an ease, a raciness and individuality in Hotspur's speech, with its interjections and broken lines, such as has not been heard before:

> Why, look you, I am whipp'd and scourged with rods,
> Nettled, and stung with pismires, when I hear
> Of this vile politician, Bolingbroke.
> In Richard's time, – what do you call the place? –
> A plague upon it, it is in Gloucestershire;
> 'Twas where the madcap duke his uncle kept,
> His uncle York; where I first bow'd my knee
> Unto this king of smiles, this Bolingbroke, –
> 'Sblood! –
> When you and he came back from Ravenspurgh.

In the early plays it is often impossible to distinguish the speech of one character from that of another, either in matter or manner; Mercutio, Romeo and Biron all have a common style, and Bolingbroke may be confused at one time with Mowbray, at another with his antithesis, King Richard. It is true that in *Henry IV* the princely houses of Northumberland and Lancaster are equally homely in their imagery, the one talking naturally in terms of wasps, ants and nettles, the other in those of bees, knives and knitting, yet there is no mistaking Hotspur for the Prince of Wales. It

Historical and Romantic Comedies

is not only the deliberation of the Prince's speech and the impetuosity of Hotspur's, his speaking thick, his explosive alliteration when angry, and his favourite expletives, 'Why' and 'A plague upon it'; it is all this of course, but the whole tone of their speech is different, and a reflection of the very different source from which each springs. In *Henry IV* it is almost true to say, for the first time, that the poetry *is* the action, the poetry *is* the character.

The finest poetry is reserved for the tragic hero, for as *Julius Caesar* is the tragedy of Brutus, 1 *Henry IV* is the tragedy of Hotspur, the only major character in the English histories whom it is possible, with but little reservation, to admire. That Shakespeare himself admired him would be clear enough, if other proof were wanting, from the fact that he makes him, again like Brutus, despise poetry, 'mincing poetry... like the forced gait of a shuffling nag', and then with characteristic and kindly irony makes him the best poet in the play. This great-hearted, generous and quarrelsome spirit is one of the most eloquent of men, yet he professes not talking; and we think of his brilliant description of Holmedon Field and the popinjay courtier, of the world of figures that he apprehends, and of his baiting of the formidably unhumorous Glendower. Shakespeare always wrote finely about war, or rather about the pageantry and circumstance of war, which appear to have stirred him deeply, and Hotspur's poetry rises to a climax as he thrills to the excitement of imminent battle:

Sound all the lofty instruments of war,
And by that music let us all embrace.

Perhaps it is the dramatic application of the sonnet music in the ringing line, 'Sound all the lofty instruments of war', that adds the final pathos to this passage and makes it so moving. Hotspur is mortally wounded, and the commonplace man triumphs; yet not altogether so: the Prince of Wales was never to speak such poignant poetry as that of the dying Percy:

> O, Harry, thou hast robb'd me of my youth!
> I better brook the loss of brittle life
> Than those proud titles thou hast won of me;
> They wound my thoughts worse than thy sword my flesh:
> But thought's the slave of life, and life time's fool;
> And time, that takes survey of all the world,
> Must have a stop. O, I could prophesy,
> But that the earthy and cold hand of death
> Lies on my tongue: no, Percy, thou art dust
> And food for –

Life ebbs with the lines, with the modulation of the labials from the proud and brilliant *b*'s and *p*'s to the softer *f*'s and *w*'s, and of the liquids from the fierce *r*'s to the gentle *l*'s. The flame leaps for the last time in 'prophesy' and 'Percy' – then brightness falls from the air.

Hotspur is Shakespeare's first real hero – 'real' in the sense that he is a character who always commands our sympathy – to talk himself completely alive in verse, yet even in *Henry IV* Shakespeare had not quite solved the problem of creating a fully dramatic medium, a verse form sufficiently natural and flexible to express both the commonplaces and the ecstasies of life with a scarcely perceptible change of tone, and without an outward flourish of style involving some violence of transition from one emotional tension to another. It is not simply that there are vestiges of the older styles, for these we should expect to find. Thus, Hotspur delivers the magnificent fustian of his speech on plucking honour from the pale-faced moon, a 'huffing part' ridiculed by Beaumont in *The Knight of the Burning Pestle*, and when the Prince reveals his policy of calculated betrayal of his friends he reverts to the lyrical vein of *Romeo and Juliet*, pursuing the theme of Sonnet 33 through a succession of subordinate clauses:

Yet herein will I imitate the sun,
Who doth permit the base contagious clouds
To smother up his beauty from the world,
That, when again he please to be himself...

When, however, Glendower falls into the sonnet poetry,

The hour before the heavenly-harness'd team
Begins his golden progress in the east,

he speaks dramatically, for it is Shakespeare's method of bringing the violent quarrel scene (III. i) to a quiet close, and the same device as that employed in *Julius Caesar* after the quarrel of Brutus and Cassius. We shall still find quibbles, 'Second to none, unseconded by you', and traces of the old poetic diction, 'ports of slumber' and 'gates of breath' for eyes and nostrils, but we shall look almost in vain for the conventional literary imagery of the earlier poetry; instead of comparisons culled from books we shall find reflections of the things that interested Shakespeare, comparisons drawn from everyday life, from the home and garden and the countryside, in particular from building, conveyancing, fruit-growing and bee-keeping – a theme that inspired the haunting line, 'The canker'd heaps of strange-achieved gold'. This is exceptional,

Whereon this Hydra son of war is born,

The Poetry of Shakespeare's Plays

but this is typical,

> Like youthful steers unyoked, they take their courses
> East, west, north, south; or, like a school broke up,
> Each hurries towards his home and sporting-place.

The death of Hotspur was a reverse for Shakespeare, and when he came to write the second part of *Henry IV* he had a struggle to recapture the dramatic verse inspired by his tragic hero. The opening scene is particularly revealing, a strange, though beautiful, episode in which he appears to be somewhat at a loss and fumbling towards his former mastery. The scene is Warkworth Castle, and as Morton approaches with the news that Harry Percy's spur is cold, Northumberland reads his message in his face:

> Yea, this man's brow, like to a title-leaf,
> Foretells the nature of a tragic volume:
> So looks the strond whereon the imperious flood
> Hath left a witness'd usurpation.

Shakespeare cannot resist the short lyrical elaboration, an image frequently met with in his work at this period, but here of little dramatic significance, and for the moment the action falters. Northumberland continues, drawing on his knowledge of Virgil:

> Even such a man, so faint, so spiritless,
> So dull, so dead in look, so woe-begone,
> Drew Priam's curtain in the dead of night,
> And would have told him half his Troy was burnt.

It is magnificent, but it is Shakespeare himself speaking, and it is Shakespeare again who echoes Sonnet 71 in the splendid

Historical and Romantic Comedies

lines with their hammering *e*'s, initial vowels, heavily reversed beat, and assonantal variation of 'unwelcome news' in 'lose... a sullen bell':

> Yet the first bringer of unwelcome news
> Hath but a losing office, and his tongue
> Sounds ever after as a sullen bell,
> Remember'd tolling a departing friend.

When at last Morton delivers his tragic message it is in the form of one of the most highly developed conceits in the plays. It begins with a fire image, which suggests, naturally enough, tempered steel, and metal suggests lead; then comes the quibbling elaboration: the steely courage of Hotspur's troops is transformed to lead by the news of his death, and as lead, because of its weight, flies quickly when propelled, so the soldiers, heavy with sorrow, fly quickly from the field. But then, their fear is light, like the supporting shaft and feathers of an arrow, so that like arrows tipped with heavy sorrow and timbered with light fear they fly swiftly towards their target, safety. Northumberland's reply is in the riddling manner of *King John*, a protracted image attenuated by paradox, quibble and antithesis, followed by an outburst of strained passion in the form of a magnificent theatrical image. To this Morton temperately replies:

> You cast the event of war, my noble lord,
> And summ'd the account of chance, before you said
> 'Let us make head.'
>
>   It was your presurmise,
> That, in the dole of blows, your son might drop:
> You knew he walk'd o'er perils, on an edge,
> More likely to fall in than to get o'er;

The Poetry of Shakespeare's Plays

> You were advised his flesh was capable
> Of wounds and scars, and that his forward spirit
> Would lift him where most trade of danger ranged:
> Yet did you say 'Go forth'.

This is something very different: a succession of short metaphors restating with variations the principal theme that Northumberland had calculated the risks of rebellion. The lines are printed here in sections to show clearly the threefold statement, and it will be observed that within each there is repetition: 'You cast the event of war – and summ'd the account of chance'. This is all dramatically relevant, and though the action moves slowly, yet it moves. It is not the uncontrolled elaboration of the early verse, but the disciplined and emphatic variation typical of the middle style.

Though much of the old declamatory rhetoric has been discarded, Shakespeare still keeps the containing framework, with its constructional devices of balance, repetition and illustration, which give precision to the periods and definition to the sense. To some extent, of course, he always retained this framework, without which the verse would fall into confusion, but after the plays of this period it becomes more sketchy, until in the tragedies it is so strained by the violent changes of pace and broken by the weight of the matter that it is scarcely perceptible, which is one reason for their greater obscurity. In these histories, however, this rhetorical structure is applied to enforcing the meaning, and is a major cause of the extreme clarity of the verse, its steadiness of movement, and its resultant epic quality. At the same time it is largely responsible for the comparative inflexibility already noticed, and a good example of this is the king's thirty-line apostrophe to Sleep in III. i, 'How many thousand of my poorest subjects Are at this hour asleep!' The structure is simple, and the development slow and logical and formal as an ode, without complexities either of undue dilation or of compression; it is, in fact, five rhetorical questions defined by a rhyming moral. In the first section Sleep is personified and invoked in a characteristic domestic image as the nurse of Nature. Internal rhyme links the first to the second section, and the second to the third, which is merely a restatement, as the fifth is of the fourth, and the whole is harmonized by the return, in the middle of the description of the storm, to the initial image of the nurse rocking a cradle.

One difference between lyric and dramatic poetry is that the one creates its own emotional tension while the other is dependent on that of the action; though it may intensify the emotion by being a little more exalted than the event, the gap must not be wide enough for the audience to be aware of the transition to a more elevated style. In this soliloquy the audience is acutely conscious that it is listening to a set piece written in a deliberately heightened and formal vein; Shakespeare is engaged with the poetry as much as with the king, whom he almost forgets in the detachment and separate development of the wind-sea image and magnificent hyperbole of the storm. Though it would scarcely be true to say that the speech is not dramatic, it is by no means fully so, and we have only to compare it with Shakespeare's treatment of the sleeplessness of Macbeth and Lady Macbeth to appreciate the difference between the 'poetic' and dramatic handling of the theme.

This noble and disciplined verse is dramatically most effective in the middle range of emotions, a range that is rarely exceeded in these plays, and it is significant that the most moving scene in 2 *Henry IV* is inspired by Hotspur: the pure and beautiful interlude of Lady Percy's appeal to Northumberland, and her panegyric of her husband, so finely set between the gross prose jesting of the Prince and Poins, and the obscenities of Falstaff and Doll Tearsheet:

> and by his light
> Did all the chivalry of England move
> To do brave acts... And him, O wondrous him!
> O miracle of men, him did you leave...

The last words that we hear her speak are, 'recordation to my noble husband'. So Lady Percy passes, a tragic figure, and perhaps the most attractive of Shakespeare's minor heroines.

Henry IV Part Two is an imperishable makeshift. Until the emergence of the reformed Prince towards the end of the play, Shakespeare was left without a hero to fill the gap between the fields of Shrewsbury and Agincourt, and had to make do with Falstaff. And how he did make do with him! – surrounding him with a pack of immortal hangers-on and dupes, Pistol, Nym, Nell Quickly, Shallow, Silence, and the less satisfactory Doll Tearsheet, until at last he was obliged to add a footnote to his epilogue, promising his eager audience to give them more of Falstaff in his next play. This, however, he found to be impossible; Falstaff was no Hotspur, and his popularity threatened to overwhelm that of the King; there was no room for them both at Agincourt, so instead of Falstaff Shakespeare gave his admirers a foretaste of the prose of his romantic comedies, Mistress Quickly's description of his death, as he went away smiling upon his fingers' ends and babbling of green fields.[1]

Henry V wears without corrival all the dignities of honour, and this was essential to Shakespeare's purpose, the writing of a play in which the epic element is pushed as far as it will go in transcending the limitations of the theatre. For the serious historical part of *Henry V* is an epic poem

Historical and Romantic Comedies

almost as much as it is a play: a series of episodes uncomplicated by plot, leading up to the climax of Agincourt, and dominated by the hero king. The narrative is related mainly by the Chorus, though by no means altogether so; in the first scene the Archbishop of Canterbury reduces the accomplishment of the two years that Henry has been king into as many minutes; Exeter tells the story of York's and Suffolk's deaths; the Constable of France and Grandpré describe the starved and ragged appearance of the English army before Agincourt, and Burgundy paints a moving picture of ravaged France. Half the verse in the play is contained in twenty speeches with an average length of forty lines, and half of these again are spoken by King Henry.

Inspired by his hero and his theme – and perhaps by Chapman's recently published translation of the *Iliad*, and the newly built Globe Theatre – Shakespeare perfected the instrument that he had forged for *Henry IV*. Neither the beautiful elaborations of his early poetry nor the equally beautiful obliquities of his later style would have been as effective a medium for an epic drama as this limpid verse of the close of the century, which so perfectly contains and so easily carries the subject. There was no hesitation, no fumbling now, as with complete confidence he gave a broader sweep and a greater resilience to the verse; now, if ever, his mind and hand went together, and the majestic torrent flowed from his pen.

The first Chorus begins in true epic fashion with an invocation of the muse, but the opening of that to Act III better illustrates, perhaps, the main qualities of the style:

The Poetry of Shakespeare's Plays

> Thus with imagined wing our swift scene flies
> In motion of no less celerity
> Than that of thought. Suppose that you have seen
> The well-appointed king at Hampton pier
> Embark his royalty; and his brave fleet
> With silken streamers the young Phoebus fanning:
> Play with your fancies, and in them behold
> Upon the hempen tackle ship-boys climbing;
> Hear the shrill whistle which doth order give
> To sounds confused; behold the threaden sails,
> Borne with the invisible and creeping wind,
> Draw the huge bottoms through the furrow'd sea,
> Breasting the lofty surge: O, do but think
> You stand upon the rivage and behold
> A city on the inconstant billows dancing;
> For so appears this fleet majestical,
> Holding due course to Harflew. Follow, follow:
> Grapple your minds to sternage of this navy...

Perhaps the most important elements in the epic style are its visual and rhythmic qualities. Nobody could read this verse without being impressed by its graphic clarity, a sequence of pictures as full of light and movement and colour (though no colour is mentioned) as a seascape by Constable or Monet, and intensified by the sound of bustle, the flapping of pennants, the creaking of canvas, and the smack of waves against the wooden hulls. Indeed, all the senses seem to be involved, and it is scarcely over-fanciful to say that one can taste, smell, and feel the tang of sea and wind. This brilliance is partly the result of the alliterative and sparkling *i*'s, culminating in the leaping 'A city on the inconstant billows dancing', a line that illustrates the vigorous and varied rhythm that so easily carries, or rather sweeps, the subject matter along. There is nothing very intricate about it; it is broad and grand like the flow of a great river, buoyant as the ships breasting the lofty surge, and yet it is a rhythm that nobody had evolved before Shakespeare. The majestic movement owes much to the overflow of the lines and the shift of the pauses within them; apart from this, the only irregularities are the initial stresses or final slacks of many of the lines, but these, in conjunction with assonance, are sufficient to give a pronounced secondary rhythm to the verse. The natural rhythm of the last two lines, for example, is essentially a falling one, and the assonance of *Harflew. Follow, follow* a prolonged echo of *furrow, billow*; and *sternage, rivage; grapple, tackle; Hampton, hempen; fanning, fancies,* etc are all similarly related. The rhythm is largely a 'false' or suggested one, induced by the redundant syllables, trochaic words and assonance.

The verse of the rest of the play resembles that of the Choruses in its ease and grace of movement, its clarity and luminosity of expression, its even distribution of simple images, its sonority of phrase and its abounding vigour. The Archbishop of Canterbury's account of the reformed king in the first scene is a good example of the style in its quieter vein, an apparently simple speech in which, nevertheless, internal rhyme and assonance are almost as complex as a passage from *The Merchant of Venice*:

> List his discourse of war, and you shall hear
> A fearful battle render'd you in music:
> Turn him to any cause of policy,
> The Gordian knot of it he will unloose,
> Familiar as his garter: that, when he speaks,
> The air, a charter'd libertine, is still,
> And the mute wonder lurketh in men's ears
> To steal his sweet and honey'd sentences.

The Poetry of Shakespeare's Plays

One cannot help pausing at the perfection of 'mute wonder lurketh in men's ears', until one realizes that it is a variation of the vowels in the second line. Did Shakespeare himself pause and consider, or was his ear so faultless that he uttered such verbal felicities 'with that easiness' described by his friends?

As a contrast there are the harsher heroics of the king's speeches, many of which might be introduced by the epic formula, 'The warlike Harry thus began to speak', and there is Canterbury's lovely allegory of the commonwealth of bees, like the early lyrical verse a poetry of adjective and phrase, but modified by the more fluid rhythm, and harmonized by the assonance based on the central 'singing', in the line that is one of the most beautiful in the poetry of this magnificent play, 'The singing masons building roofs of gold'.

There is some ado about the precise date of composition of *The Merry Wives of Windsor*, but even if it were not written immediately after *Henry V* it is a link between the histories and the romantic comedies. Not that there is anything historical about it – though the time is meant to be the early fifteenth century, it is Shakespeare's only play of contemporary English life – nor is there much romance in the very level-headed bourgeois Windsor wives and their families; but on the one hand there is Falstaff, on the other the prose of the middle comedies, an abnormal amount of it, for there is far more prose in *The Merry Wives* than in any other play. The little verse is remarkable only for one thing – Falstaff's longest speech. In *Henry IV* he speaks some dozen lines of verse, but never more than two at a time, and most of these are parodies of King Cambyses' vein or of Pistol's peculiar brand of fustian, but in the third scene of *The Merry Wives* he delivers a speech of six lines. It is true

Historical and Romantic Comedies

that it is spoken in mockery, yet it contains the most delicate line in the play, 'Sail like my pinnace to these golden shores' – most delicate, that is, if we exclude the exquisite fritters that Parson Evans makes of Marlowe, as he sings to keep up his courage. It is a very mild paradox to say that there is more poetry in the prose than in the verse, in, for example, the Host's, 'What say you to young Master Fenton? he capers, he dances, he has eyes of youth, he writes verses, he speaks holiday, he smells April and May: he will carry 't, he will carry 't: 'tis in his buttons: he will carry 't.'

Shakespeare has travelled a long way from the sophisticated and starchy Euphuism of *Love's Labour's Lost* to write prose like this, prose which, both in phrasing and rhythm, is more literary than common speech, yet not too exalted to be unacceptable on the stage as the natural everyday language of men. It is in these comedies, indeed, that Shakespeare succeeds in closing the gap between dramatic prose and verse. Even in the histories there is often an uncomfortable leap from one to the other: for example, from the familiarity of Prince Henry's prose to the formality of his verse; but with his increasing technical mastery Shakespeare was able to evolve, on the one hand, a more workaday verse, the varying rhetorical units of which resemble those of prose, and on the other a more elevated prose, the pattern of which is suggestive of verse. It is a crude over-simplification to say that in his early work Shakespeare had only two styles: the colloquial prose of low comedy and the lofty lyrical or rhetorical verse of his main themes, and that now he added two intermediate styles, the one verse, the other prose, the common frontier of which was scarcely distinguishable – yet something of this sort did happen in these comedies.

The Poetry of Shakespeare's Plays

This can easily be illustrated from *Much Ado* because of its simple stratification of dialogue, ranging from the buffoonery of Dogberry's prose to the almost tragic poetry of the Hero theme. But even at the bottom of the scale the blundering absurdities of Dogberry have a rhythm – here a succession of lengthening cadences – richer than that of ordinary speech:

> I am a wise fellow; and, which is more, an officer; and which is more, a householder; and, which is more, as pretty a piece of flesh as any is in Messina; and one that knows the law, go to; and a rich fellow enough, go to; and a fellow that hath had losses; and one that hath two gowns, and every thing handsome about him.

Beatrice's reply to Don Pedro's raillery, 'For, out of question, you were born in a merry hour', is a contrast between elegiac iambics and a leaping measure with a catch of the breath at the double stress of 'star danced':

> No, sure, my lord, my mother cried; but then there was a star danced, and under that was I born.

Socially, Don Pedro is the most distinguished character in the play, and, following Shakespeare's convention, he normally speaks in verse. His apology to Leonato illustrates the new colloquialism, verse as devoid of the poetry of Beatrice's prose as it is of the old rhetoric:

> Gentlemen both, we will not wake your patience.
> My heart is sorry for your daughter's death:
> But, on my honour, she was charged with nothing
> But what was true, and very full of proof.

The climax of the play is Hero's apparent death after being accused of unchastity, when the emotions of the audience are on tiptoe and prepared to accept, demanding even, a corresponding exaltation of poetry. Friar Francis speaks the lines that relieve the tension:

> When he shall hear she died upon his words,
> The idea of her life shall sweetly creep
> Into his study of imagination;
> And every lovely organ of her life
> Shall come apparell'd in more precious habit,
> More moving-delicate and full of life,
> Into the eye and prospect of his soul,
> Than when she lived indeed.

It is an exquisite passage, a compound of the early poetry of phrase and the parallelism of the middle style, harmonized by the echo of the first line in the last.

Thrown into relief by this dramatic dialogue on different levels, are the traces of the earlier manner; for example, the curiously archaic rhyming scene before Hero's monument (V. iii), in which Don Pedro concludes the rites with a quatrain that might come from *Romeo and Juliet*:

> Good morrow, masters; put your torches out:
>   The wolves have prey'd; and look, the gentle day
> Before the wheels of Phoebus, round about
>   Dapples the drowsy east with spots of grey.

Then Benedick's strange retort to Claudio's crudities, at the solemn moment before the restoration of Hero, is pure Bastard Faulconbridge, and quite out of character:

> Bull Jove, sir, had an amiable low;
> And some such strange bull leap'd your father's cow,
> And got a calf in that same noble feat
> Much like to you, for you have just his bleat.

Beatrice is the first of the heroines to be created out of prose – she speaks only twenty lines of verse – and yet she owes something to the poetry of Hero. Although in the gulling scene (III. i) Ursula sees her with an angler's eye, Hero instinctively endows her with the qualities of a bird, its wildness, independence, and love of life and liberty:

> For look where Beatrice, like a lapwing, runs
> Close by the ground, to hear our conference...
> I know her spirits are as coy and wild
> As haggards of the rock.

And it seems probable that the image of a bird's flight prompts the beautiful 'Disdain and scorn ride sparkling in her eye', which occurs a few lines later. Then, when Beatrice steps forward at the end of the scene to speak the sonnet-like confession of her love, she echoes Hero's image of herself as a haggard, a hawk difficult to tame,

> And, Benedick, love on; I will requite thee,
>   Taming my wild heart to thy loving hand.

This bird imagery is inseparable from our conception of Beatrice, and sweetens and freshens the somewhat stuffy atmosphere of the main plot.

There is nothing stuffy about the atmosphere of *As You Like It*. With a few trivial exceptions all the action takes place out of doors, in the country, by daylight, unaided by any magic save that of nature, and in this atmosphere the

Historical and Romantic Comedies

play is unique. The tranquil innocence of the scene – rural rather than sylvan – is suggested by the evenness of the writing, and by the impartiality with which Shakespeare distributes his poetry among the characters; the dukes speak prose as well as verse, Adam and Corin speak verse as well as prose, and though Jaques scoffs at verse he speaks one of the best-known passages in any of the plays. Then, the verse has that newly acquired ease and range that make the transition to prose scarcely perceptible, and in no other play does the prose consistently, in its beauty of phrase and rhythm, approach so near to poetry, a point that can be illustrated from the opening scene:

> My brother Jaques he keeps at school, and report speaks goldenly of his profit.
> Yet, he's gentle; never schooled, and yet learned; full of noble device; of all sorts enchantingly beloved.

It would not be easy to find adverbs more beautifully employed than *goldenly, enchantingly,* in the final cadences of these sentences.

All Shakespeare's plays are dependent on their dialogue, not so much on what is said as on how it is said, but of *As You Like It* this is true in a special sense, for its plot is too tenuous to entangle the attention of any but the least sophisticated audience. As a result Shakespeare is driven to fill in the gaps with songs, of which there are more than in any other play, to invent superfluous and loquacious characters, and to revert to his former practice of inserting set speeches, the content of which may be only remotely relevant to the action. These speeches, however, run no longer to a spontaneous lyricism, or even to rhetoric, but to a calculated didacticism or edifying allegory, couched in the lucid and expansive verse of the histories, the epic quality being subdued to a gentler pastoral note. For Shakespeare's padding of this period often takes the form of a romantic moralizing, and probably no other play has so many aphorisms, one of the main reasons for its great popularity, and perhaps the reason why it is called, with humorous irony, 'As You (the Audience) Like It'. For we, the English, are incurably romantic, and there are few things we appreciate more than sermons, sentiment, exhortation and good counsel. We like to be told how 'sweet are the uses of adversity', that 'misery doth part the flux of company', that it is bad to apply 'hot and rebellious liquors in the blood', and good to 'sweat for duty, not for meed', that 'from hour to hour we ripe and ripe', and better still, 'from hour to hour we rot and rot'; above all we like to hear that 'all the world's a stage', and to be reminded that our seventh act will be 'second childishness and mere oblivion', after which we shall make our exit 'sans everything'. Unfortunately many of us confuse the platitudes with the poetry.

This does not mean that there is no poetry in these sententious speeches; of course there is, but the poetry is not in the sentiment, it is in the words, the rhythm, and the imagery – though the imagery is not unconnected with the moralizing. Thus, the First Lord reports how Jaques moralized the spectacle of the wounded stag into a thousand similes, and true to form, Jaques himself, describing his encounter with Touchstone, says,

> When I did hear
> The motley fool thus moral on the time,
> My lungs began to crow like chanticleer.

For Jaques, like Touchstone, and indeed most of the other characters, is a great maker of similes, and it is this imagery as much as anything that evokes the pastoral scene: 'the right butter-woman's rank to market', 'as the cony', 'like a noble goose', 'as a weasel sucks eggs', 'like a doe'.

Yet there is little poetry of the highest order in *As You Like It*, and few lines that are memorable for the sheer quality of their expression – as measured, that is, by the standard of the rest of Shakespeare's work – and it is chiefly the prose that we remember, particularly the radiant prose of Rosalind in the last three acts, prose that *is* Rosalind and could not be mistaken for that of any other character in fiction.

But it is not for the prose of Beatrice and Rosalind that we have been waiting since Shakespeare wrote the last scene of *The Merchant of Venice*, it is for dramatic verse that by some miracle will be imbued with a poetry comparable to that celestial music. As soon as we hear Viola speak we know that the miracle has been accomplished; her very first words have the pure and piercing quality that we come to realize as peculiar to her speech, and we cannot read or hear without a thrill:

> *Enter Viola, a Captaine, and Saylors*
>
> *Vio.* What Country (Friends) is this?
> *Cap.* This is Illyria Ladie.
> *Vio.* And what should I do in Illyria?
> My brother he is in Elizium,
> Perchance he is not drown'd: What think you saylors?

Perhaps the strange music is imparted by the thin and clear music of the *i*'s and *y*'s, a sound that enchanted Orsino's ear:

> thy small pipe
> Is as the maiden's organ, shrill and sound.

The Poetry of Shakespeare's Plays

Partly, perhaps, it is the association of Viola with the sea, and with the sea-change suffered by so many of the later heroines. She is at once the last of the heroines of the middle comedies, and the first of those of the romances; Marina is born at sea, Perdita lost and found on the sea-coast of Bohemia, Miranda washed ashore on the magic island, and Viola cast up on the Illyrian coast.

Her first interview with Olivia begins in stilted prose, but when they are left alone and Olivia unveils, Viola unaffectedly exclaims,

> 'Tis beauty truly blent, whose red and white
> Nature's own sweet and cunning hand laid on:
> Lady, you are the cruell'st she alive,
> If you will lead these graces to the grave
> And leave the world no copy.

Here is the dramatic poetry that we have been waiting for, a poetry in which almost every word is related to character and action, and at the same time harmonically related to the other words throughout the passage. Less obvious than the earlier lyricism, because no longer static and repetitive in pattern, more natural, or more seeming-natural, therefore, and for that reason again more dramatic, it is the beginning of the perfected Shakespearean counterpoint, in which rhythm and assonance are complementary and inter-dependent, making a pattern which, though based on the linear structure, is coextensive with the speech. A reversed rhythm is suggested by *beauty truly*, emphasized by *Nature's... laid on, Lady*, and further developed by the other verbal trochees, related to them and to one another both by juxtaposition and assonance, so that this apparently simple speech is really a passage of the most intricate harmony in which almost every syllable is involved.

Historical and Romantic Comedies

Before she goes, Viola describes the depth and constancy of her own love for Orsino in terms of his love for Olivia; it is the music of the nightingale, all the liquids welling up to the climax of 'Olivia':

> Make me a willow cabin at your gate,
> And call upon my soul within the house;
> Write loyal cantons of contemned love
> And sing them loud even in the dead of night;
> Halloo your name to the reverberate hills,
> And make the babbling gossip of the air
> Cry out 'Olivia!'

Beatrice and Rosalind are creatures of prose, and their adventures much ado about nothing, but Viola is of another and a rarer element, the first of the heroines whom Shakespeare brought fully to life in verse, and he treated her predicament with a corresponding gravity. He never forgot her, and many years later was to describe the heroine of *Pericles* in terms of her of *Twelfth Night*:

>   thou dost look
> Like Patience gazing on kings' graves, and smiling
> Extremity out of act.

In another sense he never forgot her, for she is one with her poetry, and as Shylock taught Shakespeare to write dramatic verse, so did Viola teach him to write dramatic poetry. From the discipline of prose came the open epic poetry of the histories, and the easy colloquial verse of the comedies. When simplicity had been matched with flexibility, when, that is, Shakespeare had evolved a medium capable of expressing the whole range of emotions without violence, he restored the lyric element that he had used so sparingly since

The Poetry of Shakespeare's Plays

The Merchant of Venice, and wrote *Twelfth Night*. Then, after the prose and verse of the comedies of character he turned, at the beginning of the new century, to the poetry of the tragedies of character.

---

1 It is possible that Shakespeare tried to fit Falstaff into the play, but had to give his part, or some of it, to Pistol.

Part Five

TRAGEDIES OF CHARACTER AND QUASI-ROMANTIC COMEDIES

Julius Caesar, Troilus and Cressida, Hamlet, All's Well that Ends Well, Measure for Measure, Othello, Macbeth, King Lear, Timon of Athens, Coriolanus, Antony and Cleopatra.

It is generally assumed that shortly after the beginning of the seventeenth century Shakespeare suffered some profound shock to his moral nature, which occasioned this sequence of tragedies and quasi-romantic comedies, though there is nothing in the scanty records of his life at this period that offers a real clue to the nature of such a shock. In February 1601 came the Essex rebellion, in which the patron of his poems, the Earl of Southampton, was involved and sentenced to life imprisonment. If Southampton was the friend addressed in the *Sonnets* the shock would certainly be severe, and in addition, it is just possible that Shakespeare was himself disgraced because of the performance of his *Richard II* with the deposition scene on the day before the rising. But this is improbable, and no more than conjecture. His father died in September 1601, and Queen Elizabeth in March 1603, when the new sovereign, James I, released Southampton. For the rest we find Shakespeare acting in *Sejanus* in the winter of 1603 – the last record of his appearance as an actor – lodging with Christopher Mountjoy, the Huguenot tire maker, in Cripplegate, and at the same time busy with his affairs in Stratford, buying land and a cottage in 1602, tithes in 1605, and bringing two actions for debt. In 1607 his elder daughter, Susanna, married Dr John Hall, and in February 1608 his first grandchild, Elizabeth, was born. His mother died in September, and shortly afterwards he retired to New Place. There is nothing in such a background of business activity, litigation, and family affairs to suggest anything but prosperity, health, and normality of mind. But it is merely negative evidence; we know nothing of Shakespeare's friendships and loves, and we can, if we will, read into the anguish of these plays and their violent denunciations of women – denunciations that flow over into the romances – evidence of a spiritual insurrection brought about by the conduct of some woman.

Yet there are singularly few unchaste women in Shakespeare; nearly all his heroines are heavenly true, as the arrogant, stupid, suspicious and jealous lovers, husbands and fathers discover when it is too late, or almost too late, and have to retract their outrageous vilifications. Shakespeare seems to have had a greater admiration for women than for men, and to have permitted their denigration only that they might shine more brightly. He may have been unhappy when he wrote these plays, but it by no means follows that he was so; when he wrote of jealousy or ingratitude he identified himself so passionately with his theme and with his characters that for the time he *was* Othello or Leontes, he *was* Lear or Timon, and we do him an injustice if we assume that he turned to tragedy as a vehicle for the outpouring of his own misery. In any event, there is a foretaste of the familiar misanthropic and vituperative poetry some years before the writing of *Hamlet* and *Othello*:

> Let heaven kiss earth! now let not Nature's hand
> Keep the wild flood confined! let order die!
> And let this world no longer be a stage
> To feed contention in a lingering act;
> But let one spirit of the first-born Cain
> Reign in all bosoms, that, each heart being set
> On bloody courses, the rude scene may end,
> And darkness be the burier of the dead!

Tragedies of Character and Quasi-Romantic Comedies

> You seem to me as Dian in her orb,
> As chaste as is the bud ere it be blown;
> But you are more intemperate in your blood
> Than Venus, or those pamper'd animals
> That rage in savage sensuality.

The first, which might be Lear, Timon, or the world-weary Macbeth, is Northumberland in 2 *Henry IV*; the second, which might almost be Othello, is Claudio in *Much Ado*.

It is more probable that Shakespeare turned to sombre themes and tragedy because, with his acute sensitivity, he felt that popular taste was inclining that way. After all, he had to make his living by writing for the stage, the Chamberlain's company relied on him to attract audiences to the Globe, and the early years of James I's reign were a period of plague and a particularly difficult time for the theatres, so that the last words of *Twelfth Night*, 'we'll strive to please you every day', were no mere formality; the audience had to be pleased, or they would find their entertainment elsewhere. It was more than this, of course; although Shakespeare must have written with half an eye on the box office, he was an artist before he was a man of business, and having just created his first great heroine out of his patiently developed dramatic poetry the next move was as logical as it was irresistible, its application to a higher form of drama than romantic comedy.

The magnificent medium that had been evolved with such self-restraint in the histories and romantic comedies was applied to the tragedies, though with a difference. Prose was retained, but subordinated to the verse and employed only for certain well-defined purposes, so that instead of the two-thirds in the preceding period barely a quarter of these plays is in prose. Basically it is used as a contrast to the verse: for mob scenes as in *Coriolanus*, for the sub-plot as in *Lear*, for comic relief as in *Hamlet*; and it is used to distinguish madness and abnormal states of mind from sanity. Unlike the main characters of the previous period those in the tragedies normally speak prose only when the balance of their minds is disturbed: Ophelia, Lear, Timon, Othello when he falls into a trance, Lady Macbeth in the sleep-walking scene. Hamlet's use of prose is particularly interesting; he speaks verse until he tells Horatio that he will feign madness, after which he is entirely consistent, speaking prose to everybody whom he wishes to deceive, to everybody but Horatio and his mother, whom he wishes to convince of his sanity in order to redeem her. When he returns to Denmark after checking at his voyage he throws off all pretences and speaks verse, and the king knows that his opponent is far more dangerous than a madman.

Julius Caesar is exceptional in having so little prose, but then there is no madness, no sub-plot, and comic relief is confined to the mob and Casca, a character of whom we do not see enough; it is even more remarkable if it was written, as seems probable, in the middle of the prose period, shortly after *Henry V*, the open-textured epic verse of which, with its characteristic major and minor parallelisms, it resembles:

>   I will protest
> He speaks by leave and by permission,
> And that we are contented Caesar shall
> Have all true rites and lawful ceremonies.

Yet the simplicity of the English histories becomes austerity in this first essay in Roman history. Shakespeare seems to have written very carefully and with deliberate restraint, perhaps because he had a greater respect for Plutarch than for Holinshed, and took few liberties with his classical authority, perhaps because he wished the style to symbolize

Tragedies of Character and Quasi-Romantic Comedies

the asceticism of Brutus and the stoicism of Portia, even the physical spareness of Cassius. He scarcely allows himself the luxury of an image – only *The Comedy of Errors* has fewer images – and there can be no other play with so many monosyllabic lines, the effect of which is to give a remote, almost spiritual quality to the writing:

> My heart doth joy that yet in all my life
> I found no man but he was true to me...
> Night hangs upon mine eyes; my bones would rest.

And again, when to the elegiac back-tolled measure, of *ever, ever, farewell*, Brutus parts with Cassius before Philippi:

> No, Cassius, no; think not, thou noble Roman,
> That ever Brutus will go bound to Rome;
> He bears too great a mind. But this same day
> Must end that work the ides of March begun;
> And whether we shall meet again I know not.
> Therefore our everlasting farewell take.
> For ever, and for ever, farewell, Cassius!
> If we do meet again, why, we shall smile;
> If not, why then this parting was well made.

There is no elevation and flourish of style, barely the ghost of an image, and we cannot help wondering what Shakespeare would have made of this last act of *Julius Caesar* had he written in the mood and manner of *Antony and Cleopatra*, and comparing Brutus' brief dismissal of the prospect of a Roman captivity with Antony's imaginative prefiguration:

The Poetry of Shakespeare's Plays

> Wouldst thou be window'd in great Rome, and see
> Thy master thus with pleach'd arms, bending down
> His corrigible neck, his face subdued
> To penetrative shame, whilst the wheel'd seat
> Of fortunate Caesar, drawn before him, branded
> His baseness that ensued?

In *Julius Caesar* the simple style of the middle period is carried as far as it will go, but it is a superficial judgment that finds it cold and formal. Although its severity does involve some sacrifice of the overtones and infinite suggestiveness of the poetry of the later tragedies, its limitations are its virtues; it is so moving because of its understatement and unforced pitch of writing, so convincing because we are always conscious of immense reserves of power.

Like *Julius Caesar*, *Troilus and Cressida* is a difficult play to fit neatly into any scheme illustrating the development of Shakespeare's poetry, for we cannot say with any exactitude when it was written, though there can be little doubt that it was some time between *Henry V* and *Hamlet*, with both of which it has affinities. The Prologue has many echoes of the Choruses in *Henry V*, the dissertations of the Greek and Trojan warriors are, appropriately enough, on the same heroic scale as those of the Percys and Lancastrians, and their poetry has a similar epic grandeur – similar, but not quite the same; the texture of the verse is woven closer, and there is a greater complexity of expression. Compare, for example, Exeter's comment on government and an ordered hierarchy in *Henry V* with that of Ulysses:

> For government, though high and low and lower,
> Put into parts, doth keep in one consent,
> Congreeing in a full and natural close,
> Like music.

Tragedies of Character and Quasi-Romantic Comedies

> Take but degree away, untune that string,
> And, hark, what discord follows! each thing meets
> In mere oppugnancy...
> And this neglection of degree it is
> That by a pace goes backward, with a purpose
> It hath to climb.

Here Ulysses is being exceptionally compressed and elliptical, and the bulky *oppugnancy* and *neglection* give a deceptive impression of massiness and concentration, yet these Latinisms are an element of immense significance in Shakespeare's mature poetry, and first become conspicuous, overconspicuous, in *Troilus and Cressida*.

The period of the tragedies coincided with a rapid incorporation of Latin words into English, a process that was observed and commented on even in remote Cornwall. 'The long words that we borrow,' wrote Richard Carew to William Camden, 'being intermingled with the short of our own store, make up a perfect harmony, by culling from out which mixture (with judgment) you may frame your speech according to the matter you must work on, majestical, pleasant, delicate or manly, more or less in what sort you please.' He concludes with a reference to Shakespeare as an example of what he means, and Shakespeare, with his passion for words, his delight in verbal tensions, correspondences and oppositions, was of all men the most eager to make use of this addition to his wealth. But in *Troilus and Cressida* this latinized vocabulary is not always judiciously and happily employed. It is as though he suddenly became fully alive to the possibilities of these sonorous polysyllables and ponderous abstractions, and in his first enthusiasm recklessly, and just a little uncritically, exploited them: *tortive, protractive, persistive, propension, propugnation, assubjugate*. They resemble the windy words

The Poetry of Shakespeare's Plays

that Jonson in his *Poetaster* made Marston vomit up: *turgidous, ventuosity, oblatrant, obstupefact,* and it may be that this salutary satire led Shakespeare to submit himself to a similar, but voluntary, purgation. In any event, the grotesque excesses of *Troilus and Cressida* were never repeated, and the enrichment of Shakespeare's vocabulary with new latinisms was an enrichment of his poetry. Troilus' speech to Ulysses when he discovers Cressida's perfidy is a beautiful example of that intermingling of 'the long words that we borrow with the short of our own store':

> To make a recordation to my soul
> Of every syllable that here was spoke.
> But if I tell how these two did co-act,
> Shall I not lie in publishing a truth?
> Sith yet there is a credence in my heart,
> An esperance so obstinately strong,
> That doth invert the attest of eyes and ears;
> As if those organs had deceptious functions,
> Created only to calumniate.

Hamlet describes the sad face of the earth as

> this solidity and compound mass
> With tristful visage,

but it is characteristic of Shakespeare that he neutralizes this with simple words of Saxon origin, and adds,

> as against the doom
> Is thought-sick at the act.

Tragedies of Character and Quasi-Romantic Comedies

In the same way he contrasts latinisms and saxonisms in the coupled nouns of the compound image: 'this encompassment and drift of question', or sets two Saxon adjectives and their noun against Latin ones: 'Lofty and shrill-sounding throat... the extravagant and erring spirit.' Othello has 'extravagant and erring stranger', and the curious synonyms of 'exsufflicate and blown surmises'.

The 'princes orgulous' of Greece and Troy are by no means always given to magniloquence and high debate; they are very human and can relax, as when Aeneas describes the Trojans as 'debonair, unarm'd, As bending angels', and even the cynical and kingdomed Achilles can be as delicate in his imagery, seeing men like butterflies that 'Show not their mealy wings but to the summer'. Such touches of pure poetry help to unify this somewhat sprawling play by linking the scenes of war and conference to those of love. Many of these recall an earlier style; for example, the linear beauty of Cressida's

> When time is old and hath forgot itself,
> When waterdrops have worn the stones of Troy,

is reminiscent of the *Sonnets* and *Lucrece*, and the poetry of Troilus in the first scene has the vowel combinations and associations peculiar almost to *A Midsummer Night's Dream* and *The Merchant of Venice*:

> Tell me, Apollo, for thy Daphne's love,
> What Cressid is, what Pandar, and what we.
> Her bed is India; there she lies, a pearl:
> Between our Ilium and where she resides,
> Let it be call'd the wild and wandering flood,
> Ourself the merchant, and this sailing Pandar
> Our doubtful hope, our convoy and our bark.

The Poetry of Shakespeare's Plays

The poetry of these love scenes, particularly that of III. ii, strangely set in a puddle of greasy prose, so haunted Keats that he wrote, 'I throw my whole being into Troilus, and repeating those lines, "I wander like a lost soul upon the Stygian banks staying for waftage", I melt into the air with a voluptuousness so delicate that I am content to be alone'. And the rest of Troilus' speech, so Keats-like in its sensuous anticipation of taste, must have been in his mind when he wrote the Odes a few months later:[1]

> I am giddy; expectation whirls me round.
> The imaginary relish is so sweet
> That it enchants my sense: what will it be,
> When that the watery palates taste indeed
> Love's thrice repured nectar? death, I fear me,
> Swounding destruction, or some joy too fine...

The image is characteristic, for food and disease are the dominating images in *Troilus* and *Hamlet*, and as food and surfeit play an important part in the imagery of *Twelfth Night*, it may be that *Troilus* was written in the interval between the two. The supposition is strengthened by the fact that the compound image, a construction inspired by a more latinized vocabulary – 'vaunt and firstlings of those broils', 'wind and tempest of her frown' – is so prominent in *Troilus* that we seem to see in it the rapid development of the form of metaphor that is so distinguishing a feature of *Hamlet*. Then, although *Troilus* appears to have been written for private performance at an Inn of Court and has certain well-defined peculiarities, the plays have so many other features in common – a similar profusion of poetry and imagery, a similar range and variety of styles, a similar exuberance and negligence of strict form, as though Shakespeare had let himself go after the discipline and

Tragedies of Character and Quasi-Romantic Comedies

restraint of the previous period – that the splendid *Troilus* may be best accounted for as a preparation, a trial of strength, a full-dress rehearsal for *Hamlet*. There is even a similarity in the heroes, or at least in their predicaments. Shakespeare had an infallible instinct for extracting and distilling the best things from his originals; in *Troilus and Criseyde* Chaucer makes Troilus discover by accident that Criseyde has given Diomede his love token:

Than spak he thus, 'O lady myn Criseyde,
Wher is your feyth, and wher is your biheste?
Wher is your love, wher is your trouthe?' he seyde.

In Shakespeare's version, Troilus' anguished whisper is wrung from him when he overhears Cressida's treachery: 'O withered truth! O beauty! where is thy faith!' At the end of the one play Troilus is in much the same position as Hamlet at the beginning of the other. Both are disillusioned, Troilus by his mistress, Hamlet by his mother; Troilus has lost his dearly loved eldest brother, Hamlet his father. The difference is that for Troilus the way is clear.

Shakespeare was still a comparatively young man – he was only thirty-seven – when he wrote *Hamlet*, yet he was already the author of more than twenty plays, and it is, perhaps, not altogether unprofitable to speculate on the position that he might hold in English literature today had he died in the first year of the seventeenth century. Where should we place the author of *Romeo and Juliet* and *A Midsummer Night's Dream*, of *Henry IV* and *Twelfth Night* – and the *Sonnets*? If we admit, as I think we must, that even without the later tragedies and romances he still remains our greatest poet and dramatist, we get a clearer conception of the immense pre-eminence of the man who was yet to write

The Poetry of Shakespeare's Plays

Hamlet, Othello, Macbeth, Lear, Antony and Cleopatra and *The Tempest.*

Hamlet is the great landmark in Shakespeare's progress, standing like a rock, conspicuous and unmistakably defined, exactly in the middle of his career. In sheer bulk it is much the biggest of the plays; the hero is the most famous in all literature, partly because we all tend to identify ourselves with him, partly because in Hamlet we seem to come closest to Shakespeare himself; the imagery is distinctive both in form and content; it is the first of the series of great tragedies; and it is the first play in which Shakespeare's mature style is clearly revealed. All his previous work was, in a sense, a preparation for *Hamlet*; no other subject had made such demands, and it is as though Shakespeare, feeling himself at last equal to the task, decided that the time had come to show the world what he really could do.

Such a play as he conceived, a tragedy of character in which the tragic element is thrown into relief by a strain of comedy, demands every variety of verse and every diversity of speed. In the writing, therefore, he not only raised the poetry to a new pitch of tragic intensity, but drew on all the previous styles, modifying them, however, and subduing them to the theme, incorporating them in the action and in character, making them, in a word, completely dramatic, instead of employing them to fashion ornamental appendages and dazzling cadenzas.

The staple style, the norm by which all the others may be judged, is the limpid and open-textured, steady and disciplined verse of the preceding comedies and histories. This, for example, might come from *Henry IV*:

Who, dipping all his faults in their affection,
Would, like the spring that turneth wood to stone,
Convert his gyves to graces; so that my arrows,

> Too slightly timbered for so loud a wind,
> Would have reverted to my bow again
> And not where I had aimed them.

Of the slow grace of the early lyrical style there is Horatio's,

> But look, the morn, in russet mantle clad,
> Walks o'er the dew of yon high eastward hill.

Here it is dramatic, not only because the passage is short and controlled, but it is deliberately inserted to relieve the tension and to bring to a quiet close the scene of the Ghost's first appearance. The Queen's description of Ophelia's death, with its elegiac harmony of assonance and rhyme – *willow grows*, *shows*, *melodious*, etc – is a similar episode, lyrical in treatment, but intensely dramatic in its placing, the verbal music of Belmont applied to a tragic theme. Even the pedantic lyrical-gnomic style becomes dramatic – and half-humorous – on the lips of Laertes:

> The canker galls the infants of the spring
> Too oft before their buttons be disclosed.

This is the sonnet poetry, but Shakespeare characteristically adds a parallel in the current idiom:

> And in the morn and liquid dew of youth
> Contagious blastments are most imminent.

Hamlet's words to Horatio are something in the manner of the detached rhetoric that we associate with the earliest plays:

> for thou has been
> As one, in suffering all, that suffers nothing;
> A man that fortune's buffets and rewards
> Hast ta'en with equal thanks: and blest are those
> Whose blood and judgment are so well commingled
> That they are not a pipe for fortune's finger
> To sound what stop she please. Give me that man
> That is not passion's slave, and I will wear him
> In my heart's core, ay, in my heart of heart –

Hamlet begins by talking intimately to his friend, but soon appears almost to forget him and to address the audience instead. But this again is dramatic, for such a process of thought, from the particular to the general, is of the essence of Hamlet, who suddenly recollects himself and, turning to Horatio, adds, 'As I do thee. Something too much of this.'

For Hamlet, Horatio is the personification of self-control and moderation, virtues that he admires as much as he detests any form of their opposing vices: self-indulgence and excess. Thus, he loathes his uncle's debauchery and his mother's sensuality, and is offended to the soul by any intemperance of emotional display or extravagance of language, whether the verbiage of Polonius, the affection of Osric, the ranting of Laertes, or the mouthing of the players. He exalts reason as much as he deplores passion: 'How noble in reason!' is his first exclamation in his panegyric of man, 'in apprehension how like a god!' And again:

> Sure, he that made us with such large discourse,
> Looking before and after, gave us not
> That capability and god-like reason
> To fust in us unused.

Tragedies of Character and Quasi-Romantic Comedies

Yet he himself is passion's slave, and there is tragic irony in his inability to control his emotions, and pathos in his disgust at his own excesses; his fastidious nature is revolted by the way in which he unpacks his heart with words and curses, like a whore, a very drab, a scullion, and when the Ghost interrupts his almost insane onslaught on his mother he knows that it has come to chide him for being 'lapsed in time and passion'.

But Hamlet's rant is very different from the fustian of the braggarts of the early histories; it is not a sustained and monotonous fortissimo, but a controlled intensity of utterance – controlled, that is, by Shakespeare – and it is Hamlet's passionate speech, before it declines into a mere rhapsody of words, that most strikingly evinces the new element in Shakespeare's dramatic poetry. There is nothing in the earlier plays to equal the compression, intensity, and speed of this:

> Rebellious hell,
> If thou canst mutine in a matron's bones,
> To flaming youth let virtue be as wax
> And melt in her own fire: proclaim no shame
> When the compulsive ardour give the charge,
> Since frost itself as actively doth burn,
> And reason pandars will.

Or the fluid rhythm and melody of this:

> What is he whose grief
> Bears such an emphasis? whose phrase of sorrow
> Conjures the wandering stars and makes them stand
> Like wonder-wounded hearers?

The Poetry of Shakespeare's Plays

Or, in a quieter vein, there is nothing comparable to the restless imagery of his great soliloquy:

> And thus the native hue of resolution
> Is sicklied o'er with the pale cast of thought,
> And enterprises of great pitch and moment
> With this regard their currents turn awry
> And lose the name of action.

And always this heady poetry is contrasted with a slow lyrical passage. Thus Hamlet stoops from the highest pitch of his assault to,

> Save me, and hover o'er me with your wings,
> You heavenly guards! What would your gracious figure?

and the Queen follows his physical and verbal assault on Laertes with,

> Anon, as patient as the female dove
> When that her golden couplets are disclosed
> His silence will sit drooping.

For certain effects Shakespeare employs or creates a distinctive verse. Thus the Ghost speaks a solemn and spacious variety of the middle style, made strangely stiff and formal by its repetitive rhetorical structure:
> Thus, was I, sleeping, by a brother's hand
> Of life, of crown, of queen, at once dispatch'd:
> Cut off even in the blossoms of my sin,
> Unhousel'd, disappointed, unaneled...

'The Murder of Gonzago' is in archaic, sententious, and monotonous couplets, but 'Aeneas' tales to Dido' is in the

TRAGEDIES OF CHARACTER AND QUASI-ROMANTIC COMEDIES

epic manner of *Henry V*. This is generally said to be in the antiquated and turgid style of Marlowe, whose *Dido, Queen of Carthage*, written in collaboration with Nashe, contains a Virgilian description of the fall of Troy. It is certainly turgid, but no more so than Henry V's threat to the citizens of Harfleur, and there is nothing in the verse of *Dido* that approaches the rhythm of Shakespeare's,

> The rugged Pyrrhus, he whose sable arms,
> Black as his purpose, did the night resemble
> When he lay couched in the ominous horse,
> Hath now this dread and black complexion smear'd
> With heraldry more dismal...

The idiom, too, is that of Shakespeare's middle period, and the whole a fine example of the epic verse in which not only *Henry V* but much of *Troilus and Cressida* as well is written, and where, indeed, Hector's sword-play is described in terms almost identical with those of Pyrrhus'.

The peculiar imagery of *Hamlet*, its compound form and its dominant figure of disease, is noticed elsewhere, but there is another image which seems generally to escape attention, although it is curiously insistent and related to the main one – that of a gun or of a concealed explosive charge. Laertes warns Ophelia to keep out of the 'shot and danger of desire', the king compares slander's whisper to the 'poisoned shot' of a cannon, the volley of bad news to that of a 'murdering-piece', and proposes the second stratagem of the poisoned cup if the first should 'blast in proof'. Then Hamlet talks of lungs that are 'tickle o' the sere', of 'slings' or culverin, of words 'too light for the bore of the matter', and one of the most memorable images in the play is his:

The Poetry of Shakespeare's Plays

> For 'tis the sport to have the enginer
> Hoist with his own petar: and 't shall go hard
> But I will delve one yard below their mines,
> And blow them at the moon.

He has already employed the image of the sapper when he calls his father's ghost 'a worthy pioner', and Shakespeare's association of disease with mines, primarily military but by extension industrial, is made clear by Hamlet's 'ulcerous place... mining all within', and by the king's,

> But like the owner of a foul disease,
> To keep it from divulging, let it feed
> Even on the pith of life. Where is he gone?

to which the queen – quite falsely – replies,

> To draw apart the body he hath kill'd:
> O'er whom his very madness, like some ore
> Among a mineral [mine] of metals base,
> Shows itself pure.

Again, the king's simile of the murdering-piece follows immediately after a double metaphor of infection and pestilence, and his image of the gun blasting in proof is separated from that of the ulcer by only a few lines.

It is dramatically important that Claudius should be a formidable opponent; we must feel that Hamlet is confronted physically with a difficult task or his delay will make us merely impatient; the smaller the stature of the king the smaller that of Hamlet. That Claudius is an adulterer and a murderer is of the essence of the play, the main premise on which the rest depends; Hamlet calls him 'a mildewed ear', 'a vice of kings', a 'bloody, bawdy villain', but Hamlet is, to put it moderately, prejudiced, and in a less frenzied mood he calls him a 'mighty opposite'. The truth is that Shakespeare is at pains to show us the better qualities of the king; though he is a deep drinker he can carry his Rhenish and we never see him drunk; though he seduced Gertrude his love seems to be more than sensual appetite; and though he murdered his brother he tries to repent. It is not suggested that Claudius is not vicious, but he has his virtues too; he is clever, quick-witted, resolute and brave, and we must do him justice if we are to do justice to Hamlet. Shakespeare does so, and as he makes tragic heroes of Macbeth and King John by the poetry that he gives them to speak, so does he make Claudius a more worthy opponent of Hamlet:

> In the corrupted currents of this world
> Offence's gilded hand may shove by justice,
> And oft 'tis seen the wicked prize itself
> Buys out the law: but 'tis not so above;
> There is no shuffling...

The speech illustrates another quality of the poetry: the pervasive assonance, a threatening and muttered undertone of short *u*'s that runs throughout as prologue to the omen coming on. Thus, the principal assonantal sequence of Claudius – *corrupted currents, justice, shuffling, shove, above* – remarkably resembles that of Hamlet's soliloquy, two of the words, indeed, being common to both: *suffer, troubles, shuffled, undiscovered country, puzzles, currents, rub, grunt.*

As another example there is the king's,

>   the people muddied,
> Thick and unwholsome in their thoughts and whispers,
> For good Polonius' death; and we have done but greenly

The Poetry of Shakespeare's Plays

> In hugger-mugger to inter him: poor Ophelia
> Divided from herself and her fair judgment...

And in prose there is Hamlet's, 'It is such a kind of gain-giving as would perhaps trouble a woman'.

This subdued and ominous utterance is only one element in the pervading atmosphere, not so much of revenge and blood, as of mystery; another is the poetry as a whole. All poetry is mysterious both in its origin and in itself, and the greater the poetry the more moving and disturbing its remote significances and strange reverberations of meaning. But Shakespeare was himself haunted by the mysteries of life and death, and nowhere does he express this feeling more powerfully and more beautifully than in *Hamlet*, particularly, of course, in the character of Hamlet himself, and this is perhaps the main secret of the almost universal appeal of the tragic hero and his poetry.

Hamlet describes this feeling when he compares himself to a recorder, his 'mystery', of course, being very much more than his secret knowledge of his father's murder: 'You would play upon me; you would seem to know my stops; you would pluck out the heart of my mystery; you would sound me from my lowest note to the top of my compass: and there is much music in this little organ; yet cannot you make it speak.' Then, in the more powerful medium of verse:

> What may this mean,
> That thou, dead corse, again in complete steel
> Revisit'st thus the glimpses of the moon,
> Making night hideous; and we fools of nature
> So horridly to shake our disposition
> With thoughts beyond the reaches of our souls?

Tragedies of Character and Quasi-Romantic Comedies

> The dread of something after death,
> The undiscover'd country from whose bourn
> No traveller returns.

Yet Hamlet dies on a note of certitude, his assurance emphasized by the unexpected latinisms so exquisitely set between lines of homely monosyllables:

> If thou didst ever hold me in thy heart,
> Absent thee from felicity awhile,
> And in this harsh world draw thy breath in pain,
> To tell my story.

It is out of this poetry, this synthesis of lyric, epic and elegy, subdued and made dramatic, that the best-loved of Shakespeare's characters is fashioned; for by now it is axiomatic that poetry is character, and this poetry *is* Hamlet.

In the chronology of Shakespeare's plays it is usual to place *All's Well that Ends Well* soon, perhaps immediately, after *Hamlet*, though there is no external evidence to show that it was the next to be written. It is one of the plays that would have been lost but for the publication of the Folio; indeed, we should not even know of its existence, for its first mention is in the registration of that volume. Yet internal evidence suggests that some of it at least was written at about the same time as *Hamlet*, and we can scarcely read the opening of the first scene without being struck by the resemblance. It begins quietly in prose, Helena giving vent to her grief at her hopeless love for Bertram under cover of sorrow at her father's death, and her riddling first words are curiously reminiscent of Hamlet: 'I do affect a sorrow, indeed, but I have it too.' In reply Lafeu summarizes the advice of Claudius, 'Moderate lamentation is the right of the dead; excessive grief the enemy to the living', and the

The Poetry of Shakespeare's Plays

Countess that of Polonius to Laertes when she gives her blessing to her departing son:

> Love all, trust a few,
> Do wrong to none: be able for thine enemy
> Rather in power than use; and keep thy friend
> Under thy own life's key: be check'd for silence,
> But never tax'd for speech.

Shakespeare must have had *Hamlet* in mind when he wrote this, and Helena's succeeding soliloquy has the authentic texture and idiom of *Hamlet*:

> In his bright radiance and collateral light
> Must I be comforted, not in his sphere.
>   ...'Twas pretty, though a plague,
> To see him every hour; to sit and draw
> His arched brows, his hawking eye, his curls,
> In our heart's table; heart too capable
> Of every line and trick of his sweet favour.

A good deal of the rest of the verse might well be of the same period, but here the resemblance ends. In *Hamlet* the earlier styles are either fused and incorporated in the new dramatic verse, or they are made dramatic by their function, but *All's Well* is not a synthesis, it is a museum, a retrospective exhibition of styles. It might, it is true, be argued that Helena's strange speech, which so closely resembles that of the Player King in *Hamlet*,[2] is dramatic because it too is functional, because here it is incantatory, a sort of sybilline prophecy and persuasion of recovery:

> Ere twice the horses of the sun shall bring
>   Their fiery torcher his diurnal ring;

Tragedies of Character and Quasi-Romantic Comedies

>   Ere twice in murk and occidental damp
>   Moist Hesperus hath quench'd his sleepy lamp...

But the speech is not an isolated phenomenon; the play is full of antiquated couplets, and even the *Venus and Adonis* stanza, so long abandoned, reappears. Then again, when Shakespeare wishes to produce a similar effect in *Measure for Measure* he employs much more ingenious devices than pseudo-archaic couplets. When in III. i, the Duke prepares Claudio for death by persuading him that life is not worth living, he subdues him to a condition of trance by the repetitive pattern of his speech and rhythms, by the repetition of emphatic monosyllables, and by the rhyme and assonance based on the central phrase, 'The best of rest is sleep'.

Yet it is not the retrospective exhibition of styles in *All's Well* that is so surprising – Shakespeare could have written passages in his earlier manner – it is the prospective exhibition, the anticipation of a much later manner than *Hamlet*. What are we to make of this? –

>   Nay, 'tis most credible; we here receive it
>   A certainty, vouch'd from our cousin Austria
>   With caution, that the Florentine will move us
>   For speedy aid; wherein our dearest friend
>   Prejudicates the business, and would seem
>   To have us make denial.

This has all the characteristics of Shakespeare's latest and sparest style, when diction and constructions are those of ordinary speech, when rhythms bear little apparent relationship to the lines, when, in short, verse has reached the frontier of prose.

The Poetry of Shakespeare's Plays

Most of the difficulties of this unsatisfactory play can be accounted for by the fascinating hypothesis that Shakespeare in his retirement was engaged in revising an early work for publication in a collected edition, when he was overtaken by his last illness, and left it incomplete. Such an assumption would account for the confusion of styles, the numerous muddles, and, if his powers were failing towards the end, for the late manner informed only by fitful flashes of inspiration. The hypothesis is a reasonable one, for Jonson collected his works in Folio in 1616, and Shakespeare must have been well aware of his intentions; as far as we know he wrote no new work in the last two or three years of his life, but it is inconceivable that he spent all his time gossiping and drinking with Jonson, Drayton, and his Stratford cronies, and what more natural than that he should set about preparing his plays, particularly those that had not appeared in quarto, for a collected edition, handing over the work to his friends, Heminge and Condell, when he knew that he would never finish it? They almost imply this in their Preface to the Folio: 'It had bene a thing, we confesse, worthie to haue been wished, that the Author himselfe had liu'd to haue set forth, and ouerseen his owne writings... wee haue scarce receiued from him a blot in his papers.' Then, the stage directions of *All's Well*, as Sir Walter Greg points out, 'in a manner anticipate those found in Shakespeare's latest plays', when, that is, he was writing in Stratford for production in London – and it is certain that Shakespeare did not write Parolles' comment on 'your old virginity' while Queen Elizabeth was still alive, and improbable that he wrote it until some years after her death. More precisely, it is as though Shakespeare partially revised an old play about 1603, shortly after writing *Hamlet*, laid it aside, and almost completed the revision some twelve years later, the

TRAGEDIES OF CHARACTER AND QUASI-ROMANTIC COMEDIES

best poetry being that of the *Hamlet* period. There is, for example, Helena's prayer and resolve:

> O you leaden messengers
> That ride upon the violent speed of fire,
> Fly with false aim; move the still-peering air,
> That sings with piercing; do not touch my lord...
> I will be gone;
> My being here it is that holds thee hence:
> Shall I stay here to do 't? no, no, although
> The air of paradise did fan the house,
> And angels officed all.

Coleridge unexpectedly writes of Helena as Shakespeare's 'loveliest character', but if we read the most moving episode in the play, her confession of her love to Bertram's mother in I. iii, we can understand why the Countess calls her a 'maid too virtuous for the contempt of empire', and Lafeu a wife

> Whose beauty did astonish the survey
> Of richest eyes, whose words all ears took captive,
> Whose dear perfection hearts that scorned to serve
> Humbly call'd mistress.

Most of the poetry is fragmentary, a few lines, often electrifying in their intensity, thrown into brilliant relief by the comparative flatness of the surrounding writing:

> virtue's steely bones
> Look bleak i' the cold wind.

> The blushes in my cheeks thus whisper me,
> 'We blush that thou shouldst choose; but, be refused,

The Poetry of Shakespeare's Plays

>   Let the white death sit on thy cheek for ever;
>   We'll ne'er come there again.'

>   war is no strife
>   To the dark house and the detested wife.

>   but love that comes too late,
>   Like a remorseful pardon slowly carried,
>   To the great sender turns a sour offence,
>   Crying, 'That's good that's gone'.

The true successors of *Hamlet* are *Measure for Measure* and *Othello*. After the comparatively superficial and conventional treatment of moral problems in the comedies and histories, where popular aphorisms are often a substitute for originality and profundity of thought, and lyric utterance a frequent deputy for the expression of dramatic emotions, Shakespeare plunges suddenly to the centre to search the spirit of man, and examine the perilous stuff that weighs upon his heart. Even in *Measure for Measure*, in which he chooses to make all whole, Angelo has at least one quality of the tragic hero, overconfidence, and all the elements of great tragedy are there when he discovers that virtue is not proof against the assaults of virtue, as they are there in that most memorable scene in which Claudio pleads with Isabella, and a brutal and almost inhuman virtue associates itself with death to triumph over life. Such themes demand a more metaphysical language, and it is possible to make a broad distinction between the poetry written before and that written after *Hamlet*, between what may therefore be called the Elizabethan and the Jacobean poetry. The essential characteristics of the former are definition and expansion; a definition, or clarity, imparted by precision of expression, by metrical regularity, by the coincidence, absolute or approximate, of the rhetorical unit with the structural unit of the line, and by the conspicuous rhetorical framework that contains the illustrative parallelisms, images and elaborations. The Jacobean poetry is one of compression, and lacks the definition of the Elizabethan; diction becomes more personal, syntax more elliptical, there is a greater range of tone, of light and shade, a greater elasticity and variation of speed, and the structural outline loses its precision because of the increasing metrical irregularities, the disappearance of the line as the rhetorical unit, and of the bracing framework that no longer has expansive elaborations to support. The more obvious poetry of line and phrase gives place to one apparently more natural, yet more elusive, because of the extended compass of its verbal harmonies and rhythms; the texture of the verse becomes correspondingly complex, its colour at once richer and more sombre, the quality of its music deeper and more sonorous. In terms of the visual arts, the Elizabethan poetry resembles the work of the early Florentine painters, the Jacobean resembles that of Rembrandt. *Hamlet* shares the characteristics of both styles, and it is in *Measure for Measure* and *Othello* that the new Jacobean poetry is first heard almost throughout.

This darker and intenser hue and greater mellowness of tone are partly the result of the more philosophical diction, of the abstract latinisms that are no longer merely decorative or eccentric, as in *Troilus and Cressida*, but a completely assimilated and essential element in Shakespeare's expression, though frequently they are set in sharp and deliberate contrast to vivid images couched in native idiom, as when Isabella so lightly tells Claudio that 'tomorrow you set on', for the only remedy is one not to be thought of:

The Poetry of Shakespeare's Plays

> *Isab.* Yes, brother, you may live:
> There is a devilish mercy in the judge,
> If you'll implore it, that will free your life,
> But fetter you till death.
>   *Claud.*   Perpetual durance?
>   *Isab.* Ay, just; perpetual durance, a restraint,
> Though all the world's vastidity you had,
> To a determined scope.
>   *Claud.*   But in what nature?
>   *Isab.* In such a one as, you consenting to 't,
> Would bark your honour from that trunk you bear,
> And leave you naked.

Then consider Claudio's agonized plea for life, the latinisms isolated and cut off by rhyming and chiming Saxon monosyllables, the tremendous impact of 'obstruction' instead of 'grave', and the added poignancy of 'motion' for the concrete but inert 'body':

> Ay, but to die, and go we know not where;
> To lie in cold obstruction and to rot;
> This sensible warm motion to become
> A kneaded clod; and the delighted spirit
> To bathe in fiery floods, or to reside
> In thrilling region of thick-ribbed ice;
> To be imprison'd in the viewless winds,
> And blown with restless violence round about
> The pendent world.

The means and the effect are similar in the terrible anguish of Macbeth's cry,

>   this my hand will rather
> The multitudinous seas incarnadine,
> Making the green one red.

Tragedies of Character and Quasi-Romantic Comedies

Claudio's speech illustrates another element that gives a particular richness to this early Jacobean poetry, the romantic adjectives so heavily charged with remote and haunting associations: 'thrilling region of thick-ribbed ice', Cassio's 'gutter'd rocks and congregated sands', and Othello's 'antres vast and deserts idle', lines that probably inspired Milton when he wrote in *Comus*, 'airy tongues that syllable men's names On sands and shores and desert wildernesses'.

It is in *Othello* that Shakespeare's dramatic poetry comes to full maturity. Though we would not have it shorter, *Hamlet* is too long as a stage play, relevance is tenuous at times, and there is some dissipation of the emotions, but in *Othello* every speech bears on the centre, every line is directed like a shaft with unerring precision towards the catastrophe, and not only character, but the conflict as well, is reflected in the speech of the protagonists. Iago's is typically broken into short exclamatory units and twisted into parentheses, or it glides into a smooth and sickening mock morality:

> But he that filches from me my good name
> Robs me of that which not enriches him
> And makes me poor indeed.

His imagery is drawn from the sea – 'another of his fathom', 'give him cable' – but more often, and this is the dominating imagery of the play, from animals, either stupid or vicious – 'like his master's ass', 'As salt as wolves in pride'. Othello speaks with a majestic, oceanic rhythm that is the surface movement of his emotional depths, the token of his confidence and the nobility of his nature. His speech is not, as Iago has it, 'horribly stuff'd with epithets of war', though there is some truth in his gibe that it is inflated 'with a bombast circumstance'. Othello is the only hero in Shakespeare without a sense of humour,[3] and it is this deficiency that is in part responsible for those lofty flights that in anybody with less essential simplicity and sincerity would become magniloquence, as it is part of the tragic frailty that makes him so vulnerable to Iago's attack. His images, elemental and romantic, have a corresponding grandeur, though he sometimes tempers his exalted style with the most prosaic of illustrations:

> when light-wing's toys
> Of feather'd Cupid seel with wanton dulness
> My speculative and officed instruments,
> That my disports corrupt and taint my business,
> Let housewives make a skillet of my helm;

and he can achieve the same effect of nobility and power in a monosyllabic line devoid of imagery: 'Keep up your bright swords, for the dew will rust them.'

But when jealousy and mistrust have corrupted his integrity, when his faith in Desdemona falters, and Iago pours in the poison of his dusty periods, the monumental alabaster of his verse is sullied with obscenities, and crumbles into the broken rhythms and bestial imagery of his adversary. Iago secures Desdemona's handkerchief, and, as he sees Othello approach, utters the beautiful and terrible incantation,

> Not poppy, nor mandragora,
> Nor all the drowsy syrups of the world,
> Shall ever medicine thee to that sweet sleep
> Which thou owedst yesterday.

Tragedies of Character and Quasi-Romantic Comedies

The lines might be Othello's and prologue to his heartbroken farewell to content of mind and the pride of war, for he speaks in the third person – 'Othello's occupation's gone' – as though he had lost not only happiness but himself as well, as indeed he has. There is, at this critical juncture, a strangely dramatic confusion of tongues, as though Iago were momentarily inspired to speak the poetry of Othello, and Othello reduced to the sententious moralizing of Iago; coming from the lips of Iago this would be malicious mockery, but spoken with all sincerity by Othello the effect is shocking:

> He that is robb'd, not wanting what is stolen,
> Let him not know't and he's not robbed at all;

and shocking too is the fall from his lofty valediction to the brutal directness of Iago, 'Villain, be sure thou prove my love a whore'.

There is a resurgence of splendid poetry when Othello swears to be revenged on Desdemona and Cassio, but it is cold and stubborn with hate; the iterated *c*'s and hammering *on*'s give it the inexorable motion of some monstrous machine, and the qualifying of every noun with an adjective imparts a steady, menacing rhythm, until the plunge into the gulf of 'Swallow them up':

>   Like to the Pontic sea,
> Whose icy current and compulsive course
> Ne'er feels retiring ebb, but keeps due on
> To the Propontic and the Hellespont;
> Even so my bloody thoughts, with violent pace,
> Shall ne'er look back, ne'er ebb to humble love,
> Till that a capable and wide revenge
> Swallow them up.

The Poetry of Shakespeare's Plays

It is barely credible that only four hundred lines separate Othello's 'Perdition catch my soul, But I do love her' from his final 'Damn her, lewd minx! O damn her!' Yet such is the brilliance of the writing in this scene (III. iii), perhaps the most terrible in all literature, that there is no effect of strain and improbability; on the contrary, the deception and damnation of Othello appear inevitable when he is exposed to the diabolical cleverness of Iago.

The scene could not have been written in prose; it could not have been written by Shakespeare himself before this period; it is the verse, or rather it is Shakespeare's mature dramatic poetry that carries audience and reader into another and rarer atmosphere, where sea-level critical faculties are blunted, emotions are stimulated and abnormally sensitive, and time folds up like a fan. This is also true of the ensuing tragedies, particularly of *Macbeth* and *Lear*, and in *Othello* Shakespeare secures a further dramatic effect from his medium. 'To be once in doubt is once to be resolved', Othello had said when his torment began. This is almost, but not quite true; there is a period of doubt in which he pitifully tries to cling to his belief in Desdemona's innocency, and this is reflected by his speaking prose, prose that alternates between a savage imprecation and a lyrical cry:

> Let her rot, and perish, and be damned tonight... O, the world hath not a sweeter creature: she might lie by an emperor's side, and command him tasks... Hang her! so delicate with her needle: an admirable musician... But yet the pity of it, Iago! O, Iago, the pity of it... I will chop her into messes: cuckold me!

The partial recovery of his noble utterance is an ominous indication that his period of uncertainty is almost over, and it is the grandeur of his language as he looks at the sleeping Desdemona that makes it so terrible, for it means that he is no longer a man divided against himself, that belief in her guilt has triumphed over his conviction of her innocence; he is resolved, and sublimely and pitifully convinced of the justice of his cause. All that is noble in his nature is once again revealed in his lyrical soliloquy with its threefold *cause*, its fivefold *light* and tragic pun; like a fountain it mounts on the solid column of the monosyllables, and falls in the splendid cadences of *monumental alabaster, flaming minister, cunning'st pattern of excelling nature*:

> It is the cause, it is the cause, my soul:
> Let me not name it to you, you chaste stars!
> It is the cause. Yet I'll not shed her blood,
> Nor scar that whiter skin of hers than snow
> And smooth as monumental alabaster.
> Yet she must die, else she'll betray more men.
> Put out the light, and then put out the light:
> If I quench thee, thou flaming minister,
> I can again thy former light restore,
> Should I repent me: but once put out thy light,
> Thou cunning'st pattern of excelling nature,
> I know not where is that Promethean heat
> That can thy light relume.

Desdemona saw Othello's visage in his mind, quite transfigured by the nobility of his nature; more directly, we can see Othello's mind in his poetry.

A belief in a natural order was at the root of Shakespeare's philosophy: an order in which the singing stars and planets revolve with a patent majesty about the earth, where season follows season with a rhythm comparable to the rising and falling of the tides or the breaking of waves on the shore, and where the lower animals are subject to man, a pattern that is repeated in the regulation of society, from the small constellation of the family to the great galaxy of the nation as a whole. Nature is order and harmony, and it is natural for subjects to obey their rulers, for children to obey their parents; disorder and discord are unnatural, and revolution, murder, and filial disobedience are the beginnings of chaos and the elements of tragedy. It is this theme of unnaturalness that is common to the tragedies of this period, from *Hamlet* to *Coriolanus*. The first three treat of murder; in *Hamlet* of 'most unnatural murder. Murder most foul, as in the best it is, But this most foul, strange, and unnatural.' Hamlet cannot kill himself, much less kill a king in cold blood, and before he goes to upbraid his mother he prays that his heart will not lose its nature, that he may speak daggers but use none, that he may be cruel without being unnatural. And consider the dialogue when the swelling seed of doubt first flaws Othello's defences:

> *Oth*. And yet, how nature erring from itself –
> *Iago*. Ay, there's the point: as – to be bold with you –
> Not to affect many proposed matches
> Of her own clime, complexion and degree,
> Whereto we see in all things nature tends –
> Foh! one may smell in such a will most rank,
> Foul disproportion, thoughts unnatural.

In *Macbeth* one of the keywords is 'unnatural': 'unnatural, even like the deed that's done', 'unnatural deeds do breed unnatural troubles', and when Macbeth revisits the witches he calls for the chaos that must be the outcome of his unnatural actions:

Tragedies of Character and Quasi-Romantic Comedies

> Though you untie the winds and let them fight
> Against the churches; though the yesty waves
> Confound and swallow navigation up;
> Though bladed corn be lodged and trees blown down;
> Though castles topple on their warders' heads;
> Though palaces and pyramids do slope
> Their heads to their foundations; though the treasure
> Of nature's germins tumble all together,
> Even till destruction sicken; answer me.

The poetry is assuming yet wider functions; not only is it character and action, it is also the impalpable and peculiar atmosphere that envelops a Shakespearean tragedy, investing it with a yet greater intensity and significance.

Macbeth is the supreme example of a play that ascends the brightest heaven of tragic invention by virtue of its poetry. Here Shakespeare was confronted with the task of making a tragic hero out of a regicide and assassin, almost of making a Hamlet out of a Claudius. It is true that Macbeth's degeneration into a bloody tyrant is in a sense beyond his control, one crime leading inevitably to another, and the inexorability of this step by step corruption prevents the complete withdrawal of our sympathies; yet he becomes 'a devil more damned in evils' than any in hell, 'smacking of every sin that has a name'. If this were all, the play would be a tragedy without a hero, but Macbeth retains our sympathy in spite of his actions, by his speech, by his poetry, and all other emotions are overwhelmed by a great compassion as we listen to the tragic music of his latest musings. Romeo, Hamlet, Othello, Lear, Antony have no need of poetry to make them into tragic heroes, though it is their poetry that gives them their stature; but a prosaic and heroic Macbeth is an impossibility.

The Poetry of Shakespeare's Plays

The range of Macbeth's eloquence is as wide as Othello's, from the simplest of monosyllabic lines to those of grand and resounding polysyllables, but whereas Othello is always – except for the brief periods of his derangement and the discovery of his error – lucid and icy-clear, the master of his imagination, his imagery the unruffled reflection of his thought, Macbeth is a pipe for his imagination's finger to play upon, his expression more complex and much more various. His emotional states are reflected in the rhythms of his speech, from the horrible gliding and dipping movement of,

>   wither'd murder,
> Alarum'd by his sentinel, the wolf,
> Whose howl's his watch, thus with his stealthy pace,
> With Tarquin's ravishing strides, towards his design
> Moves like a ghost,

to the monotonous and hopeless beat of,

> And all our yesterdays have lighted fools
> The way to dusty death;

from the spacious and generous measure in which he speaks of Duncan,

>   his virtues
> Will plead like angels trumpet-tongued against
> The deep damnation of his taking-off,

to the agitated motion and turbid imagery of,

> My thought, whose murder yet is but fantastical,
> Shakes so my single state of man that function

Tragedies of Character and Quasi-Romantic Comedies

Is smother'd in surmise, and nothing is
But what is not.

The last lines illustrate one way in which the strange and unnatural atmosphere is suggested – the enigmatic 'nothing is but what is not', and similar riddling antitheses run throughout: 'lost and won', 'fair is foul', 'fathered yet fatherless', 'welcome and unwelcome things'. All is doubt and uncertainty; the witches are and are not, daggers and bloody hands appear in the air, dead men walk and woods remove, and even the day is a delusive twilight. Language has lost its innocence, and the simplest words assume a sinister ambiguity; Macbeth promises to make his wife *joyful* with the news of Duncan's approach, and she tells him that their royal guest must be *provided for*. Even the loveliest poetry is ominous, and Duncan comments on the beauty of the scene as he approaches the castle which he enters as a murdered man. The imagery adds to the horror – and no other play has such a wealth of imagery – for much of it is derived from the commonest everyday objects, so that they too are tainted and suspect, and no more to be trusted than men or words; thus, the grooms' daggers are breeched with gore, night strangles the travelling lamp, and on the night of the murder 'there's husbandry in heaven, their candles are all out'.

The scene is one of a suffocating confinement; cut off from the world by the castle walls, by the impalpable barriers of fog and the nebulous obstruction of fear, the potential victims of Macbeth are trapped, and he himself 'cabin'd, cribb'd, confined, bound in' to his own doubts and fears. This atmosphere of confinement, congestion and obstruction is intensified by the poetry itself, not by the words and imagery alone, but by the syllables and letters as well, by the dramatic employment of alliteration and

The Poetry of Shakespeare's Plays

assonance. In the first great speech of the play Lady Macbeth invokes 'thick night', and solicits the powers of darkness to stuff her with cruelty, to block all entrances to pity, and to envelop her with evil:

> fill me, from the crown to the toe, top-full
> Of direst cruelty! make thick my blood,
> Stop up the access and passage to remorse...

The keyword is 'thick', and the process of thickening, clotting' and coagulation is intensified by the repetition of the *k* in words which thereby become associated with it, by the alliterative hard *c*'s, and by the muffled vowels of *Duncan, dunnest, blood*, etc, suggestive also of cruelty and of the blanketing fog and smothering surmise of the earlier scenes. She returns to a similar phraseology and literation when she goads Macbeth into murdering Duncan – 'I have given suck...milk...pluck...screw...stick' – but the murder of Banquo is the work of Macbeth alone, and how sinister is his repetition of her invocation of night and of an almost identical language. Perhaps no passage in Shakespeare better illustrates his power of accentuating horror by its association with beauty:

> ere the bat hath flown
> His cloister'd flight; ere to black Hecate's summons
> The shard-borne beetle with his drowsy hums
> Hath rung night's yawning peal, there shall be done
> A deed of dreadful note... Come, seeling night,
> Scarf up the tender eye of pitiful day,
> And with thy bloody and invisible hand
> Cancel and tear to pieces that great bond
> Which keeps me pale! Light thickens, and the crow
> Makes wing to the rooky wood...

Tragedies of Character and Quasi-Romantic Comedies

It is one of the subtlest touches in this play that is so full of dramatic irony that when Macbeth is told that his wife is 'troubled with thick-coming fancies' he asks the doctor if he cannot 'cleanse the stuff'd bosom of that perilous stuff that weighs upon the heart'.

In *King Lear*, *Timon of Athens* and *Coriolanus* the theme of unnaturalness is pursued into the wider realm of ingratitude, the ingratitude of children to father, of friends to benefactor, of a people to its saviour; 'Is there any cause in nature that makes these hard hearts?' Lear asks, and Timon, 'Does... all mankind show me an iron heart?' The subject was one that moved Shakespeare deeply, more deeply perhaps than any other, and these three plays are unparalleled in the violence of their vituperative and denunciatory poetry.

It is the scale of *Lear* that makes it the most sublime of all Shakespeare's plays; not only kings and princes, but gods and the elements themselves are involved in the titanic struggle, the imaginative action of which covers the space between the cracked vault of heaven and the monstrous depths of the sea, and experience ranges from the mystery of birth to that of the grave. 'Thou know'st', says Lear to Gloucester,

> When we are born, we cry that we are come
> To this great stage of fools,

and Edgar concludes Lear's unfinished preaching,

>   Men must endure
> Their going hence, even as their coming hither:
> Ripeness is all.

The Poetry of Shakespeare's Plays

Then, the play moves, if not with the speed of *Macbeth*, yet with a greater momentum, because of its greater weight, or as Coleridge has it, 'like the hurricane and the whirlpool, absorbing while it advances', and leaving destruction and death in its wake. Lear himself is of more than mortal proportions, and in our imagination looms large as legend out of the vague and uncertain immensities of the desolate scene. Old age and the wrongs that he endures add to his stature, but chiefly it is the volcanic utterance of his passions that gives him his almost megalithic dimensions. The tremendous scale of the play is the product of the poetry.

Lear's terrible imprecation as he stands exposed to the fury of the storm illustrates this. Macbeth was prepared to sacrifice the world to secure his own ends, but Lear implores the elements to crush it, to make general the sterility that he has already invoked upon his ungrateful daughters, to make cosmos less than chaos, to make it *nothing*, the most significant word in the play:

> Blow, winds, and crack your cheeks! rage! blow!
> You cataracts and hurricanes, spout
> Till you have drench'd our steeples, drown'd the cocks!
> You sulphurous and thought-executing fires,
> Vaunt-couriers to oak-cleaving thunderbolts,
> Singe my white head! And thou, all-shaking thunder,
> Smite flat the thick rotundity o' the world!
> Crack nature's moulds, all germins spill at once
> That make ingrateful man!

The verse can scarcely contain the violence of the passion, and like Lear's mind is itself on the point of disintegration under the strain. The first line consists of eight monosyllables, six of which are powerfully stressed, and throughout the speech almost every syllable calls for emphasis. All the verbs are Saxon monosyllables, their impact concentrated at the beginning or end of the lines, and monstrous forces are suggested by the massive polysyllabic nouns and compound adjectives, and by the spondaic character of the verse in which the strange splitting sound of thunder is heard – *smíte flát the thíck; cráck náture's móulds*. It is the poetry, a harmonized cacophony, of the frame of things beginning to disjoint. Yet this poetry is more than a symbol, more in the nature of metaphor than simile, an identification rather than a parallel; it is at the same time Lear on the verge of madness and it is the storm, a representation, an equivalent far more terrifying and convincing than any man-made imitation in a playhouse. Shakespeare did not rely on noises off, lighting, and other distracting apparatus for the atmosphere that he wished to create. He wrote it.

In a sense, the whole action of the play is a storm, the tempest in Lear's mind, reaching its full force in the physical fury of the scenes on the heath, its still centre in the episode of Cordelia's reconciliation, rising again in the disaster of defeat, and subsiding into a sullen and wintry silence on the death of Lear. Everywhere its pitiless ferocity makes itself felt in the violence of the verbs; even in the quietest scene of all, IV. iii, Kent explains how shame so elbows, stings and burns Lear that he dares not meet Cordelia. And it is as a body in torment that his anguished mind is reflected in the imagery; thus, Cordelia's most small fault 'like an engine wrenched' his 'frame of nature from the fixed place', when he wakes to a precarious sanity he is still bound upon a wheel of fire, and he dies stretched out upon the rack of this tough world.

Perhaps nothing better illustrates the immense range of Shakespeare's genius and his complete mastery of his medium than the death of Lear:

The Poetry of Shakespeare's Plays

> And my poor fool is hang'd! No, no, no life!
> Why should a dog, a horse, a rat, have life,
> And thou no breath at all? Thou'lt come no more,
> Never, never, never, never, never!
> Pray you, undo this button: thank you, sir.
> Do you see this? Look on her, look, her lips,
> Look there, look there!

What other writer could make great tragic poetry out of monosyllables, dogs and rats and buttons, and a fivefold 'never'?

After writing *Lear* Shakespeare turned to North's translation of Plutarch's *Lives of the Noble Grecians and Romans* for inspiration, or at least for the plots of what are probably his next three plays, *Timon*, *Coriolanus*, and *Antony and Cleopatra*. But *Timon* was never finished, and that Shakespeare should have abandoned it is understandable, for Timon is not really a tragic hero; he is the victim neither of circumstance nor of a single error of judgment, but of consistently foolish extravagance, and though, as Hazelton Spencer puts it, his fall might 'stir the emotions of a susceptible millionaire', there can be few others who feel deeply for his fate or have much patience with his misanthropy. The difference between the true tragic hero and the false is well illustrated by Othello and Timon; 'One that loved not wisely but too well', Othello says of himself; 'Unwisely, not ignobly, have I given', is Timon's complacent self-censure. The one was unwise but not foolish, the other both unwise and foolish; moreover, Othello is the victim not only of his own unwisdom but of the maleficent Iago, whereas Timon is the victim of his own foolishness in spite of the beneficent Flavius.

But it is to *Lear* that *Timon* is most closely linked, both by its main theme and its subordinate elements. The

Tragedies of Character and Quasi-Romantic Comedies

overgenerous Timon is driven by the ingratitude of his friends to misanthropy and suicide, as Lear is driven by the ingratitude of his daughters to misanthropy and madness. Then, as Gloucester is both a parallel and a foil to Lear, so are Apemantus and Alcibiades to Timon; they are complementary, for it is the professional cynic, Apemantus, who voices the misanthropy that Alcibiades, banished by an ungrateful Senate, has as much justification for feeling as Timon. Flavius, the faithful servant, corresponds to Kent, but there is no heroine, no Cordelia, in *Timon*.

Though many of the qualities of *Lear* are found in *Timon*, the same verbal violence and a similar imagery, it follows from the lack of hero and heroine that the poetry of the two is not strictly comparable, for much of the significance and energy of the poetry in *Lear* derives from the characters who speak it, whereas in *Timon* they can add little to it; the one is poetic drama in the highest degree, the other little more than a dramatic poem. Yet there is magnificent poetry in *Timon*, particularly in IV. iii, most of it vituperative, like Timon's prayer that women may depopulate the world, but some of it half lyrical, as in his address to the gold, the 'bright defiler of Hymen's purest bed' that corrupts like woman. Then, and perhaps again because of the tenuous relationship between language and character, a strange immediacy, an almost personal, autobiographic note creeps in. Although the episode is satirical, the poet's description of his art in the first scene may be Shakespeare's comment on his own inspiration and mode of composition:

> Our poesy is as a gum, which oozes
> From whence 'tis nourish'd: the fire i' the flint
> Shows not till it be struck; our gentle flame
> Provokes itself, and, like the current, flies
> Each bound it chafes.

The Poetry of Shakespeare's Plays

There is a similar intimacy of touch in Timon's criticism of painting, and in the servant's beautiful and compassionate speech in IV. ii, as though Shakespeare had himself recently experienced the shame of apparent ingratitude in abandoning a comrade to the grave:[4]

> As we do turn our backs
> From our companion thrown into his grave,
> So his familiars to his buried fortunes
> Slink all away; leave their false vows with him,
> Like empty purses pick'd; and his poor self,
> A dedicated beggar to the air,
> With his disease of all-shunned poverty,
> Walks, like contempt, alone.

But the most moving as well as the most significant thing in the poetry of *Timon* is the sea. Although the earlier plays abound in allusions to, descriptions of, and imagery drawn from the sea, it is never of primary importance to the action, and there are very few scenes in which it is a visible presence; there is the murder of Suffolk in 2 *Henry VI* and the shipwreck of Viola on the coast of Illyria, but the arrival of Othello and Desdemona in Cyprus is described, and the episode on Dover cliff in *Lear* is make-believe. In *Timon*, however, the sea imagery leads up to the sea itself, and we feel something of the thrill experienced by Xenophon and the Ten Thousand when they reached the summit of Mount Theches and saw the Black Sea at their feet, for it is with the sea that the poetry of Shakespeare's final period is imperishably associated. Plutarch tells us simply that Timon 'died in the city of Halae, and was buried upon the seaside', but Shakespeare expands this note into a pervasive imagery, and even makes of it a significant dramatic theme. Timon is 'sick of this false world', and it is this sickness that makes

Tragedies of Character and Quasi-Romantic Comedies

him choose 'the very hem o' the sea' for his retreat and for his grave. 'Thou shalt build from men', he enjoins Flavius, and to himself he says,

>   Then, Timon, presently prepare thy grave;
>   Lie where the light foam of the sea may beat
>   Thy grave-stone daily.

And his last words are,

>   Timon hath made his everlasting mansion
>   Upon the beached verge of the salt flood;
>   Who once a day with his embossed froth
>   The turbulent surge shall cover.

The same sea music is heard again when Alcibiades speaks his valediction:

>   yet rich conceit
>   Taught thee to make vast Neptune weep for aye
>   On thy low grave, on faults forgiven.

There is nothing comparable to this in *Coriolanus*, a play in which the poetry quite fails to create the atmosphere that is such an important element in Shakespearean tragedy, as it fails to make a tragic hero of Coriolanus. The two are not unrelated, for had Shakespeare been able to identify himself with the upright Coriolanus as he did with the erring Macbeth, he might have invested him with a similar poetry that would have compelled our compassion, but even he seems to have been chilled by his hero, whose inflexible arrogance alienates our sympathies and brings upon himself a fate that we cannot feel is wholly undeserved. The poetry lacks the richness and depth, the all-important connotations and overtones of the other tragedies; it is poetry in a void, and starts no echoes. That Shakespeare's heart was not greatly in the matter is suggested by his mechanical use of North, even in the central speech of the play, when Coriolanus throws himself on the mercy of his old enemy and proposes an alliance against Rome. North's version of Plutarch reads,

> I am Caius Marcius, who hath done to thy self particularly, and to all the Volsces generally, great hurte and mischief, which I cannot denie for my name of Coriolanus that I beare. For I never had other benefit nor recompence, of all the true and paynefull service I have done and the extreme daunger I have bene in, but this only surname: a good memorie and witnes, of the malice and displeasure thou showldest beare me.

This Shakespeare translates into verse with the minimum of effort:

> My name is Caius Marcius, who hath done
> To thee particularly, and to all the Volsces,
> Great hurt and mischief; thereto witness may
> My surname Coriolanus: the painful service,
> The extreme dangers, and the drops of blood
> Shed for my thankless country, are requited
> But with that surname; a good memory,
> And witness of the malice and displeasure
> Which thou shouldst bear me.

North's prose has a sustained nobility and dignity, but it rarely flashes into poetry; certainly it does not do so here, and Shakespeare's verse rendering adds nothing of inspiration. It is true that he does better than this in Volumnia's great speech of intercession, breaking down North's generalities

Tragedies of Character and Quasi-Romantic Comedies

into vivid detail, and integrating it by working in the leading themes, but to compare Shakespeare's use of North in *Coriolanus* with that in *Antony and Cleopatra* is at once to become aware of the difference between a dramatic poetry that means little more than it says and one that means so much more, and to recognize the vital part played by the pervasive overtones that make the peculiar and indefinable atmosphere in Shakespeare's greatest plays.

North describes Antony's first meeting with Cleopatra, and 'the manner how he fell in love with her':

> She disdained to set forward otherwise, but to take her barge in the river of Cydnus; the poop whereof was of gold, the sails of purple, and the oars of silver, which kept stroke in rowing after the sound of the music of flutes, howboys, citherns, viols, and such other instruments as they played upon in the barge. And now for the person of her self...

It is a fine passage, yet North's prose is only the beginning of Shakespeare's poetry:

> The barge she sat in, like a burnish'd throne,
> Burn'd on the water: the poop was beaten gold;
> Purpose the sails, and so perfumed that
> The winds were love-sick with them; the oars were silver,
> Which to the tune of flutes kept stroke and made
> The water which they beat to follow faster,
> As amorous of their strokes. For her own person,
> It beggar'd all description...[5]

North secures his effect without the aid of imagery, yet, as Mr Middleton Murry has shown, it is Shakespeare's imagery that articulates and gives a new significance to

THE POETRY OF SHAKESPEARE'S PLAYS

North's description, by representing the winds, the water, and the air as overcome with love for Cleopatra. Not only this, however; by his alterations and additions Shakespeare creates another harmony even more penetrating.

This water music is a poetry of the labials so favoured by Shakespeare in his early work, *p, b, v, f, w, m*, interwoven with the rich vowels and rhythms of his maturity. By adding *burnish'd, burn'd on, her own*, he extends and enhances the assonance of *purple, person*, a sequence to which *poop* and *tune of flutes* is related by the addition of *perfumed*. North makes no mention of 'water', but Shakespeare contrives *water...follow faster...fancy outwork nature*, all of them words which by their position in the line induce a counter-rhythm, so that the verse is interpenetrated and harmonized by assonance and a secondary measure, each of which is dependent on the other for its full emphasis and extension. It is only in *Antony and Cleopatra* that Shakespeare brings this counterpoint to perfection, by the full exploitation of the redundant syllable and mid-line pause.

The interpenetration of the play by harmonizing elements is carried much further than this. There is the imagery, 'of vastness generally', images not only of physical immensity, as in 'Whate'er the ocean pales, or sky inclips', but also of the vastness of love and time, as in Cleopatra's 'Eternity was in our lips and eyes', and 'I have immortal longings in me'. Then the speeches achieve their full significance only in relation to the play as a whole. The description of Cleopatra on Cydnus is no mere decorative interlude; it is deliberately set in the middle of the Roman scenes, so that, like the strange invisible perfume that emanated from her barge, her spirit is powerful even in the capital of the empire, and her charms envelop Antony in the house of Caesar. In the same way, Antony, although physically absent, is kept always before us in Alexandria,

Tragedies of Character and Quasi-Romantic Comedies

where all the talk is Antony, and it is only after his death that Cleopatra gives us the picture that is companion to that drawn by Enobarbus of herself:

> His legs bestrid the ocean: his rear'd arm
> Crested the world: his voice was propertied
> As all the tuned spheres, and that to friends;
> But when he meant to quail and shake the orb,
> He was as rattling thunder. For his bounty,
> There was no winter in't; an autumn 'twas
> That grew the more by reaping: his delights
> Were dolphin-like; they show'd his back above
> The element they lived in: in his livery
> Walk'd crowns and crownets; realms and islands were
> As plates dropp'd from his pocket...
> But if there be, or ever were, one such,
> It's past the size of dreaming.

These must be among the noblest lines ever written, and they illustrate very well the way in which the phrase is dependent on the passage for its complete perfection, as the passage is dependent on the play. For example, the beauty of the phrase, which so perfectly describes Shakespeare as well as Antony, 'his voice was propertied as all the tuned spheres', depends partly on the sequence, *sovereign, propertied, dolphin, dropped, pocket*, partly on that of *man, sun, moon, tune*, and partly on the more important one of *dreamed, sleep, reared, spheres, reaping, hearing, dreaming*. Even words, or rather certain syllables, permeate the play with their peculiar music, and are themselves enriched by their association; thus *arm* in the first line is an echo of some of the most prominent and most highly charged words in the poetry: *charm, chare, Mars, marble, star, dark, darkling, garland, remarkable*, and it is not by mere accident that the

The Poetry of Shakespeare's Plays

proper names, *Mark Antony* and *Charmian* are so frequently repeated.[6] Coleridge called *Antony and Cleopatra* by far the most wonderful of Shakespeare's historical plays, and this is but a modest assertion, for it has claims to be considered the most wonderful play of all. In what is probably the last of his tragedies, Shakespeare perfected the form that had been the object of all his previous endeavour, a play completely integrated by his poetry, a whole in which each unit is a significant and inseparable part of a larger member.

A period of seven or eight years separates the writing of *Hamlet* from that of *Antony and Cleopatra,* and during this period Shakespeare's progress had been always towards a greater flexibility of expression, towards a verse that could be expanded and contracted, accelerated and retarded at will, a verse that was capable of the dramatic expression of any action, any idea, and any emotion, from the most trivial to the most tragic. The process involved a rejection of conventional syntax, an extension of vocabulary by the incorporation and invention of new words ('captious and intenible sieve'), the pressing of old ones into strange uses, the distillation of language until all superfluous matter had been expelled and only its essence remained:

>   not the imperious show
> Of the full-fortuned Caesar ever shall
> Be brooch'd with me...
> Your wife Octavia, with her modest eyes
> And still conclusion, shall acquire no honour
> Demuring upon me.

Then technically it involved a development of all the devices that modify the standard rhythm: foot substitution, the redundant syllable, and those that modify the length of the

TRAGEDIES OF CHARACTER AND QUASI-ROMANTIC COMEDIES

rhetorical unit as well, enjambment and the mid-line pause, that is, the pause *anywhere* within the line. Shakespeare had almost mastered this complete flexibility by the time he began *Antony and Cleopatra*, but there was at this juncture a striking and rapid advance, as though suddenly he had quite clearly seen his goal and made a spurt to achieve it. Particularly striking is the development of enjambment by the employment of light and weak endings, those barely stressed monosyllables, pronouns and auxiliaries, prepositions and conjunctions, that hasten the overflow of one line into the next, breaking down the last barrier of the verse form, and yielding yet another source of impetus and energy.

Lines like these could not have been written before this period:

>   I must be laughed at,
> If or for nothing or a little, I
> Should say myself offended, and with you
> Chiefly i' the world; more laugh'd at, that I should
> Once name you derogately, when to sound your name
> It not concerned me.

In *Antony and Cleopatra* language is no longer a heap of words to be built up in lines according to rules of prosody and syntax; it is kneaded into a sculptor's medium, a plastic substance to be modelled into forms of any shape or size. The last speech in the play is a good example of the spareness to which Shakespeare could reduce this verse, a poetry devoid of ornament, devoid of imagery, and stripped to the structural elements of verb and noun, a poetry of rhythmically and harmoniously related words, in which the dactylic measure of *monument, Antony, funeral, solemnity,* is repeated and varied in the light endings of *story is, glory which, army shall*:

The Poetry of Shakespeare's Plays

>   Take up her bed,
> And bear her women from the monument:
> She shall be buried by her Antony:
> No grave upon the earth shall clip in it
> A pair so famous. High events as these
> Strike those that make them; and their story is
> No less in pity than his glory which
> Brought them to be lamented. Our army shall
> In solemn show attend this funeral,
> And then to Rome. Come, Dolabella, see
> High order in this great solemnity.

The wonder of this great poetry is its Cleopatra-like quality of infinite variety; at one moment it is as abstract and austere as this speech of Caesar's, at another massy and fraught with imagery, and then it swells and broadens into the slow movement of Cleopatra's elegiacs:

> O, wither'd is the garland of the war,
> The soldier's pole is fall'n: young boys and girls
> Are level now with men; the odds is gone,
> And there is nothing left remarkable
> Beneath the visiting moon.

Shakespeare can do anything with language; there is no forcing of it now, and at the most poignant moments he rejects the aid of the emotional feminine ending and relies on the simplest words and rhythms:

> Unarm, Eros; the long day's task is done,
> And we must sleep.

> Finish, good lady; the bright day is done,
> And we are for the dark.

TRAGEDIES OF CHARACTER AND QUASI-ROMANTIC COMEDIES

In her panegyric of Antony, Cleopatra can make a climax out of plates and pockets, which by all the rules should be the profoundest bathos, and when she dies Charmian makes tragic poetry out of 'Your crown's awry'. North nobly describes the death of Charmian:

> One of the soldiers, seeing her, angrily said unto her: 'Is that well done, Charmion?' 'Very well,' said she again, 'and meet for a princess descended from the race of so many noble kings.' She said no more, but fell down dead by the bed.

This Shakespeare accepts with little alteration; with little alteration, but with the addition of two transfiguring words:

> It is well done, and fitting for a princess
> Descended of so many royal kings.
> Ah, soldier!

It is strange, yet not so strange, that *Antony and Cleopatra* should have been neglected for more then two centuries in favour of Dryden's tinkling imitation, *All for Love*, and that even today it is relatively little known. The most perfect of the tragedies, its poetry is the most splendid that Shakespeare ever wrote, but once he had brought a dramatic form to perfection it was not his custom to repeat it; *The Merchant of Venice* is followed by *Henry IV*, *Twelfth Night* by *Hamlet*, and having written the crowning glory of *Antony and Cleopatra* he turned from romantic tragedy to romantic tragi-comedy, and applied the golden poetry of his prime to *Pericles*.

The Poetry of Shakespeare's Plays

1. cf. *Nightingale*: My heart aches, and a drowsy numbness pains My sense.
   Melancholy: burst Joy's grape against his palate fine.
2. Full thirty times hath Phoebus cart gone round
   Neptune's salt wash and Tellus' orbed ground...
3. Though we never hear Macbeth make a jest, we feel quite sure that he could, and even Coriolanus can call his wife 'my gracious silence'. It is difficult to imagine Othello being trivial.
4. His fellow actor, Augustine Phillips, died in May 1605, leaving legacies to most of the company.
5. It is worth comparing this with Dryden's version in *All for Love*.
6. As in I. v, for example. Shakespeare loved to incorporate proper names in his verse, either in Homeric catalogue, as in *Henry V*, or as part of his dramatic design, as in 'Desdemona, Desdemona! dead!', or for their euphony and felicitous combination with ordinary words! as 'Farewell! Othello's occupation's gone'.

Part Six

ROMANCES

Pericles, Cymbeline, The Winter's Tale, The Tempest.

About the time of the completion of *Antony and Cleopatra*, events occurred that seem to have had an important influence on Shakespeare. Early in 1608 his grandchild, Elizabeth Hall, was born at Stratford; then a few months later he became one of the original shareholders in the Blackfriars theatre taken over by his company, the King's Men, who engaged the rising dramatists, Beaumont and Fletcher, to write for them. The last two events are related, for the Blackfriars was a small, roofed theatre, the greater intimacy and more exclusive audience of which called for a quieter style of acting and a quieter style of play than those to which the groundlings of the Globe and the other public theatres had long been accustomed. Beaumont and Fletcher had each written separately for the boys' company that had occupied the Blackfriars before the King's Men took it over, and they now began their collaboration in the new genre of tragi-comedy, starting probably with *Philaster* in 1608 and lasting until Beaumont's marriage and retirement in 1613, when for *Henry VIII* and *The Two Noble Kinsmen* Fletcher found a collaborator in Shakespeare. The period of the Beaumont and Fletcher collaboration in tragi-comedy for the King's Men at the Blackfriars exactly coincided, therefore, with that of Shakespeare's preoccupation with the same, or a similar type of play, and the question arises as to who was the originator. There are resemblances to *Philaster* in *Cymbeline*, and it may be that Shakespeare owed something to the younger men; on the other hand we cannot be sure which came first, and it is probable that *Pericles* preceded both.

The Poetry of Shakespeare's Plays

All these plays have a common theme, the trials and misfortunes, almost tragic and often humiliating, of a young heroine; but Shakespeare's have a further peculiarity: they are all concerned with the relationship of father and daughter, the first three with the restoration of a lost daughter to her father, and it is neither unreasonable nor sentimental to see in this some connection with Shakespeare's renewal of ties with Stratford, with his daughter's marriage, the birth of his granddaughter, and his preparations for retirement to New Place. The importance of Elizabeth should not be underestimated, for she was the only grandchild of Shakespeare born in his lifetime. The early death of his only son precluded his establishing a Shakespeare family in Stratford, but that he set great store on perpetuating his line is clear from the terms of his will, in which he entailed all his real property on his elder daughter Susanna Hall and her heirs male, failing whom it was to pass to her daughter Elizabeth.

It is, of course, possible that Shakespeare simply gave the public what it wanted. *Hamlet* was undoubtedly a great popular success, and just as the great series of tragedies that sent all London flocking to the Globe to see Burbage in the title parts may have been an exploitation of this success, so when the Blackfriars venture had to be made a profitable undertaking he may have changed his manner to attract a wealthier audience to its more expensive seats. No doubt there is some truth in this explanation, but it is unlikely that it is by any means the whole truth. After writing *Antony and Cleopatra* he was ready for a change of dramatic form, and a new theme was already working in his head, so that when his fellow actors and shareholders, and his own self-interest, urged him to write something new for the Blackfriars stage, he was not unprepared, and turned readily from the tragedies of old and middle age to the romance and courage of youth, and the love of father for daughter.

Up to a point it is a return to the middle comedies, as though Shakespeare took up the romantic theme where he had left it at *Twelfth Night*. Here are the loyal and innocent young heroines – Marina, indeed, is very close to Viola, and has her poignant purity of speech ('silver-voiced', Pericles calls her):

> I am a maid,
> My lord, that ne'er before invited eyes,
> But have been gazed on like a comet: she speaks,
> My lord, that, may be, hath endured a grief
> Might equal yours, if both were justly weighed.

Here are the familiar comic characters, Autolycus, Stephano, Trinculo, and here again are the incomparable songs and lyrics. Yet it is Illyria with a difference, a scene over which the tremendous actions of the tragedies have passed and left their impress, a scene modified by their passions, their evil and nobility, their anguish and heroism, and the reader experiences a strange sensation as he re-enters it; he recognizes the well-known landmarks, but it is a country transported to another climate, there is a different light, an atmosphere that may perhaps best be described as one of spring in autumn.

This peculiar atmosphere can partly be accounted for by the contrast in age between the main characters, father and daughter, for all these heroines, except Imogen, are much younger than those of the middle comedies, and we follow their fortunes from birth. The babe theme is a new element, and Miranda's discovery of a brave new world is the fulfilment of the blessing invoked by Pericles on the sea-born Marina, 'this fresh-new sea-farer'.

The Poetry of Shakespeare's Plays

Then again, the humour of these plays is very different from that of *Twelfth Night* and *As You Like It*. The comic characters are all those of low life, even the delightful shepherd and his son in *The Winter's Tale*; there is no middle and no courtly comedy, no Falstaff, Sir Toby, Jaques, no Beatrice and Benedick, no Rosalind and Orlando. The comedy is a boisterous relief from the much graver treatment of the main themes, for there is more evil in any one of these romances than in the tragedies of *Coriolanus* and *Antony and Cleopatra*, and there are passages in *Cymbeline* and *The Winter's Tale* that read almost like *Othello* or *Lear*. This is where Shakespeare's tragi-comedies differ from those of Beaumont and Fletcher; theirs are neither right tragedy nor right comedy, but, as it were, a weak compound of the two, superficial affairs of misfortune, sweet pathos and indecency, but Shakespeare's have the elements of real tragedy, and tragic situation and character are sharply contrasted with the genuinely comic. Marina suffers the very real agony of the brothel, and there can be few critics today who question the authenticity of these scenes in *Pericles*. Shakespeare saw life whole, steadily and unflinchingly, and understood and sympathized with what he saw because the range of his mind was coextensive almost with that of man, embracing thoughts and emotions the rarest and most spiritual as well as those at the other extreme most earthy and physical. Nor did this vast range imply any dissipation of energy, a compensating tenuity; he lived more intensely along the whole gamut of experience than do most men within their much more modest limits. He is not a moralist in the usually accepted sense of the word, and it seems never to have occurred to him to select from life and to emphasize only the good and the beautiful; instead he opposes virtue with vice, reveals glimpses of the basest desires in the noblest of men, puts a gross jest into the mouths of his purest heroines, and introduces his loveliest poetry with an obscene quibble – consider Cloten's instructions before the song, 'Hark, hark, the lark', for example. He is the bawdiest of the Elizabethan dramatists, and yet he is the chastest, for his obscenities are spontaneous and witty as his images, with which indeed they are intimately associated, never the conventional and snickering innuendoes of Fletcher and so many of his contemporaries, or they are a reflection of life transformed by his art into something strangely pathetic or richly humorous. They do not contaminate, and no amateur of pornography will find much salacious satisfaction in his works. The horrors of the Mytilene bawdy-house are genuine enough, but so is the ring of Shakespeare's incomparable humorous prose: 'The nobleman would have dealt with her like a nobleman, and she sent him away as cold as a snowball, saying his prayers too.'

Even the songs seem to have been modified by their contact with tragedy. The lyrics of the earlier comedies, with the exception of *Twelfth Night*, are little more than musical interludes, those of *As You Like It* little more than music-hall turns. In the tragedies, however, the songs spring, or seem to spring, naturally from the action, and are used with supreme art to emphasize the pity, most of them – those of the Fool in *Lear*, the snatches of Ophelia, the Willow Song of Desdemona – being popular ballads of the day, and all the more effective for their familiarity. Although the sophisticated Jacobean audience of the private theatres demanded song, dance and spectacle as essential ingredients in their entertainment, the lyrics of the romances, once again Shakespeare's composition, have the dramatic spontaneity of those in the tragedies; Autolycus sings because he must, and Ariel's songs are the sweet airs of the island, the music that crept by Ferdinand upon the waters.

The Poetry of Shakespeare's Plays

And it is the sea as much as anything that gives the peculiar and enchanting atmosphere to the romances. It first assumes importance in *Twelfth Night*, where the imagery is a constant reminder of its proximity; in *Timon* it is a presence and a theme, but in *Pericles* it bursts upon us with the full force of a hurricane; we are ourselves at sea in the storm in which Marina is born. Throughout the garbled text of the first two acts we have been straining to catch the authentic Shakespearean note, but there is no mistaking it when it comes, in the movement and music of Pericles' prayer, the great confident wave-like sweep of the verse thundering through the last lines in unbroken trochees:

> Thou god of this great vast, rebuke these surges,
> Which wash both heaven and hell; and thou, that hast
> Upon the winds command, bind them in brass,
> Having call'd them from the deep! O, still
> Thy deafening dreadful thunders; gently quench
> Thy nimble sulphurous flashes!

It is the prelude to a greater tempest still.

The sea – and flowers. Flowers are inseparable from Jacobean tragi-comedy, and Fletcher was an adept at exploiting the pathos of his heroine's predicament by means of a poetry of flowers, pressing, as it were, the pathos out of the flowers and their associations rather than out of the words. In *Pericles* and *Cymbeline* there are traces of this device, and an occasional faint flavour of Fletcherian over-sweetness, as when Marina goes to strew violets and marigolds on her nurse's grave, and Arviragus promises to sweeten Imogen's sad grave with primroses, harebells and eglantine. Then there is the embarrassing episode when Imogen, mistaking the headless Cloten for Posthumus, digs a grave with her 'poor pickaxes' – Fletcherian phrase – and covers the body with leaves and flowers. It is true that, in spite of a certain confusion, most of the flowers are those of spring; even Cymbeline's queen, whom we might expect to brew her poisons out of hemlock, nightshade and yew, gathers violets, cowslips and primroses, and Iachimo so far forgets his chambering nature as to call the sleeping Imogen 'fresh lily', and to compare the mole on her breast to 'the crimson drops i' the bottom of a cowslip'. But in *The Winter's Tale* the treatment of flowers is very different, and quite free from the taint of Fletcherian sentiment; Autolycus breaks into the picaresque ballad of 'When daffodils begin to peer', and after distributing the flowers of middle summer, Perdita calls for

> Daffodils
> That come before the swallow dares, and take
> The winds of March with beauty.

There is a freshness, a virility, in this poetry of spring beyond the scope of Fletcher, yet it is noticeable that in *The Tempest* Shakespeare seems deliberately to avoid any poetry of flowers – there is one mention in the masque, and Ariel's 'In a cowslip's bell I lie' – and the nearest approach is Gonzalo's moving appeal as the ship splits, 'Now would I give a thousand furlongs of sea for an acre of barren ground, long heath, brown furze, any thing'.

These four plays are all further removed from reality than the middle comedies. *Cymbeline* is the only one that can strictly be classed as a Jacobean tragi-comedy; *Pericles* is more in the nature of a fairy story, and *The Winter's Tale*, thrice referred to as 'an old tale', so 'that the verity of it is in strong suspicion', is on the confines of the greatest fairy tale of all. Perhaps when writing *The Winter's Tale* Shakespeare smiled to himself as he confused even more than usual his chronology and geography, wildly mingling Christian cults with those of Apollo, one moment invoking the gods and the next laughing at Puritans, giving Hermione the Emperor of Russia for her father, and Julio Romano for her sculptor. It was Robert Greene who first located Apollo's oracle on the isle of Delphos and gave Bohemia a sea-coast, but Shakespeare adopted these errors, to the horror of Ben Jonson, and further confounded the matter by reversing the kingdoms of Leontes and Polixenes. How disastrously far from the spirit of these plays the would-be realist producer may err is well illustrated by Charles Keans' tidily antiquarian revival of a hundred years ago. In this a classical era was faithfully reproduced; Sicily at the height of its glory, the romantic Bohemia became the classical Bithynia, Time was exalted to Cronos, and the sheep-shearing scene to a Dionysiac Festival; by judicious cutting it was possible to introduce a Pyrrhic dance and 'an allegorical tableau of Luna and the Stars (personified)', and if the production was really consistent we must believe that, instead of 'lavender, mints, savory, marjoram, the marigold that goes to bed with the sun', Perdita distributed 'the vegetation peculiar to Bithynia, adopted from the private drawings of George Scharf, Esq., FSA, taken on the spot'.

It follows from this fairy-tale atmosphere that there is a comparative lack of definition in the characters; most of them are either shadowy or scarcely credible creations, important only as they work out the story and speak the poetry, stock figures who do not really determine the action, and are inconsistent when the action demands it. Though Shakespeare is as careful as ever in the portrayal of his heroines, we neither know nor care much about their lovers, Florizel, Ferdinand, Lysimachus the frequenter of brothels, and Posthumus, 'the loyal'st husband that did e'er plight troth', who wagers on his wife's chastity, introduces the would-be seducer, accepts his word, and orders her murder. Then, consider for a moment Cloten, the clotpoll whose head Guiderius sends rolling seawards down the steam. He *is* a clotpoll, everybody says so: 'a thing too bad for bad report', 'a puttock', 'a fool', 'an ass that cannot take two from twenty and leave eighteen', and yet he can speak with some authority and send the Romans about their business, and he talks of gold like Timon:

> 'Tis gold
> Which buys admittance; oft it doth; yea, and makes
> Diana's rangers false themselves, yield up
> Their deer to the stand o' the stealer.

There are exceptions, notably Prospero, Hermione, and the excellent Paulina, but it is as foolish to write pages of solemn analysis of the characters of Cymbeline and his Queen, Pericles and Leontes, as of Bluebeard and Cinderella.

As T E Lawrence rejoiced in the freedom that he found after resigning the responsibilities of his Arabian campaign, so Shakespeare, after the tremendous strain of the tragedies, seems to have welcomed a less exacting dramatic form in which character was of secondary importance, and which afforded him the chance of writing an equivalent of the lyric poetry that he had renounced after *The Merchant of Venice*. As far as we know, the only non-dramatic poetry that he had written since then was *The Phoenix and Turtle* and possibly some of the *Sonnets*, but in the last tragedies, from *Timon* onwards, there are signs of a desire to revert to the purer poetry of his youth, particularly in the imagery, as when Coriolanus greets Valeria as

The Poetry of Shakespeare's Plays

> The moon of Rome; chaste as the icicle
> That's curdied by the frost from purest snow
> That hangs on Dian's temple.

And almost the whole of *Antony and Cleopatra* is poetry in which the lyric element is carried as far as it will go without detracting from the essentially dramatic quality of the verse. But when Florizel describes Perdita's hand,

> As soft as dove's down and as white as it,
> Or Ethiopian's tooth, or the fann'd snow that's bolted
> By the northern blasts twice o'er,

Shakespeare is writing the poetry of *A Midsummer Night's Dream*:

> That pure congealed white, high Taurus' snow,
> Fann'd with the eastern wind, turns to a crow
> When thou hold'st up thy hand.

Again, when Prospero says to Miranda, 'The fringed curtains of thine eye advance', and Cerimon exclaims as he revives the almost lifeless Thaisa, he has returned to the emblematic imagery of his earliest poetry:

> Her eyelids, cases to those heavenly jewels
> Which Pericles hath lost, begin to part
> Their fringes of bright gold: the diamonds
> Of a most praised water do appear
> To make the word twice rich.

Iachimo's description of the sleeping Imogen is the companion to that of the sleeping Lucrece:[1]

>   fresh lily!
> And whiter than the sheets! That I might touch!
> But kiss; one kiss! Rubies unparagon'd,
> How dearly they do't! 'Tis her breathing that
> Perfumes the chamber thus: the flame o' the taper
> Bows toward her, and would under-peep her lids
> To see the enclosed lights, now canopied
> Under these windows, white and azure, laced
> With blue of heaven's own tinct.

The imagery and the conceits are the same, but there the resemblance ends. The verse of *Lucrece* is that of an apprentice, all its simple and easily comprehended beauty lavishly displayed on the surface, but the labour and experience of twenty years lies concealed in the verse harmonies and rhythms of *Cymbeline*, and it is this wedding of the early lyricism to the mastery of maturity that, as much as anything, gives the strange atmosphere of spring in autumn to the romances. The poetry does not run away with the dramatist as in the early days; it does not deviate into an irrelevant lyricism, it expands when it is dramatically justified, as in Pericles' lament for Thaisa:

> A terrible childbed hast thou had, my dear;
> No light, no fire: the unfriendly elements
> Forgot thee utterly; nor have I time
> To give thee hallow'd to thy grave, but straight
> Must cast thee, scarcely coffin'd, in the ooze;
> Where, for a monument upon thy bones,
> And aye-remaining lamps, the belching whale
> And humming water must o'erwhelm thy corpse,
> Lying with simple shells.

The Poetry of Shakespeare's Plays

When Julia in *The Two Gentlemen of Verona* decides to follow Proteus she invents an allegory, but when Imogen decides to meet Posthumus – though 'decides' is scarcely the word since it implies deliberation – she calls for a horse with wings and, her heart in a panting plight, inquires in her breathless poetry how far it is 'to this same blessed Milford'.

It is probable that over no other play of Shakespeare have critics so violently disagreed as over *Cymbeline*. Johnson's comment is well known:

> This play has many just sentiments, some natural dialogues, and some pleasing scenes, but they are obtained at the expense of much incongruity. To remark the folly of the fiction, the absurdity of the conduct, the confusion of the names and manners of different times, and the impossibility of the events in any system of life, were to waste criticism upon unresisting imbecility, upon faults too evident for detection, and too gross for aggravation.

But for Hazlitt, '*Cymbeline* is one of the most delightful of Shakespeare's historical plays... Dr Johnson is of opinion that Shakespeare was generally inattentive to the winding-up of his plots. We think the contrary is true.' Sir Walter Raleigh quotes Johnson with approval, and adds, 'The best and highest part of Shakespeare's imagination was not concerned, one is tempted to say, with plot-architecture'; Sir Arthur Quiller-Couch exclaims as he closes the play, 'O mighty craftsman!' Critics disagree, too, about the characters, though most of them are at one over Imogen, who was almost idolized in the nineteenth century, most deliriously and iambically by Swinburne, who found in this 'play of plays... the woman best beloved in all the world of song and all the tide of time'. But Hazelton Spencer, the

American scholar, will have none of these things; not only is the plot tedious, Imogen uninteresting, and the rest of the principal characters 'unmitigated bores', but there is scarcely any poetry in the play outside the song, 'Hark, hark the lark', and the first stanza of 'Fear no more the heat o' the sun'.

Then there is the vexed question of the vision and 'ludicrous scroll' in the last act, both of which even the cautious Sir Edmund Chambers rejects as a spectacular theatrical interpolation. On the other hand, Bernard Shaw roundly maintained that 'the act is genuine Shakespeare to the last full stop', saved by the comic jailor and the masque, if handsomely produced, from being 'a tedious string of unsurprising *dénouements* sugared with insincere sentimentality after a ludicrous stage battle'. Despite jailor and masque, however, the play 'goes to pieces in the last act', and he rewrote it, retaining 89 lines of Shakespeare's text and substituting some 300 of his own for the 700 odd that he scrapped. It must be admitted that the compressed Shavian anti-romantic version is more entertaining than the diffuse Shakespearean romantic; Posthumus does not forget that Iachimo owes him ten thousand ducats, Arviragus relieves himself of years of accumulated irritation at Belarius' moralizing, Iachimo turns out to be a wit instead of a garrulous bore, and the disillusioned Imogen, instead of embracing Posthumus with the determination never again to be shaken off, comments sourly, 'I must go home and make the best of it As other women must'. 'That's all I ask', replies the impenetrable Posthumus.

More entertaining than Shakespeare; but better than Shakespeare? With mock artlessness Shaw tells us how easy he found it to write Shakespearean blank verse, but he does not claim to be able to write Shakespearean poetry with the same ease. It is true that the last act is not remarkable for its

The Poetry of Shakespeare's Plays

poetry; Shakespeare was himself more than a little bored by the business of unravelling the threads he had so light-heartedly tangled, by 'this fierce abridgement' as Cymbeline with unconscious irony calls it, and like any other poet he did not write his best when bored. Nevertheless, as Shaw would probably have been the first to admit, the best poetry in his version is the 89 lines of Shakespeare. It is not only that we miss such things as Cymbeline's comment on his dead queen's treachery,

>   Mine eyes
> Were not in fault, for she was beautiful,
> Mine ears that heard her flattery, nor my heart
> That thought her like her seeming; it had been vicious
> To have mistrusted her;

we miss the inimitable movement of the great verse flashing with imagery, we miss, in short, the poetry. Shaw's verse is as limpid as his prose, but it runs thin and shallow. Here is his description of the battle; he talks big, but there is no weight:

> Their horsemen trot in order to the charge
> And then let loose th' entire mass full speed.
> No single cavaliers but thirty score
> As from a catapult four hundred tons
> Of horse and man in one enormous shock
> Hurled on our shaken legions.

And here is Shakespeare's:

>   Then began
> A stop i' the chaser, a retire; anon
> A rout, confusion thick: forthwith they fly

Chickens, the way which they stoop'd eagles; slaves,
The strides they victors made; and now our cowards,
Like fragments in hard voyages, became
The life o' the need; having found the back-door open
Of the unguarded hearts, heavens, how they wound!

The verse of *Pericles* is simple and open-textured as becomes its romantic theme, and so is that of much of *Cymbeline*, but sometimes with a sudden snake-like contraction, convulsion almost, it closes on itself, shedding all ornament and leaving little but the essential sinews of its structure. Thus, when Iachimo first meets Imogen, he asks himself expansively,

What, are men mad? Hath nature given them eyes
To see this vaulted arch and the rich crop
Of sea and land, which can distinguish 'twixt
The fiery orbs above and the twinn'd stones
Upon the number'd beach, and can we not
Partition make with spectacles so precious
'Twixt fair and foul?

'What makes your admiration?' Imogen asks, and Iachimo continues:

It cannot be i' the eye; for apes and monkeys,
'Twixt two such shes, would chatter this way and
Contemn with mows the other: nor i' the judgment;
For idiots, in this case of favour, would
Be wisely definite: nor i' the appetite;
Sluttery, to such neat excellence opposed,
Should make desire vomit emptiness,
Not so allured to feed.

The compression of this is unequalled even in *Antony and Cleopatra*, and such a violent change of pace and tension is unexpected in a comedy, as, indeed, Shakespeare intended it to be, for it is leading in to Iachimo's obscene and circumstantial fabrications of Posthumus' debauchery. But it is a kind of writing which, carried much further, will cease to be the language of romantic comedy.

There was always the danger that the speed and profusion with which Shakespeare's imagination presented him with ideas and images would lead to a private language, or at least to one too personal for the theatre. In the early plays this was averted by his delight in words for their own sakes and a consequent elaboration of equivalents, in the plays of the middle years by a disciplined repetition and parallelism, but after the tragedies, when architectural verse form had been squeezed into a free sculptural one, and the medium itself reduced to a condition of plasticity, the verse was so sensitive that any abnormal pressure was liable to upset its formal relationships and impair its coherence. Like the statues in a pediment or stained-glass figures in a clerestory window, the language of poetic drama to be fully effective on the pedestal of the stage must be larger than life and simpler in form and outline. Shakespeare nearly always magnificently achieves this clarity of pattern, but not always in *The Winter's Tale*, the tragic part of which supplies just that pressure which leads to some confusion and distortion.

The Winter's Tale is not really a tragi-comedy, it is a tragedy and a comedy. By the end of Act III Leontes has brought about the deaths of his wife, his son and his daughter, only to find that he has been mistaken in his 'wretched fishing jealousies', and his speech, concluding, 'Come and lead me to these sorrows', might be the conclusion of a five-act tragedy. But it is only the beginning of the comedy, or rather of the romance, and it is probable that for most people *The Winter's Tale* means, not the wintry story of the first three acts, but the sheep-shearing scene, which has more than once been abstracted and made into a short play of Florizel and Perdita, almost it might be said to mean the first two hundred lines, almost, indeed, the flower speech of Perdita:

> O Proserpina,
> For the flowers now, that frighted thou let'st fall
> From Dis's waggon! Daffodils...

Daffodils, like a bow drawn at the end of the short line, followed by the leaping swallow flight and the breathless *beauty*;[2] the shy withdrawal of *violets dim*, suggested by the sudden drop to the monosyllable and thin vowel; the whole bound together by the interplay of the short and long *i*'s, by the assonance of *flowers, swallow, sweeter, sweet friend, strew him*, and by the more prolonged echo of phrases, 'take the winds of March', 'lack to make you garlands'. There is little poetry of such crystalline purity outside this idyllic episode, but here it is only part of the exquisite lovemaking, and Florizel replies,

> when you do dance, I wish you
> A wave o' the sea, that you might ever do
> Nothing but that; move still, still so,

and then,

> And own no other function: each your doing,
> So singular in each particular,
> Crowns what you are doing in the present deeds,
> That all your acts are queens.

The Poetry of Shakespeare's Plays

Perhaps the shadow of the watchful Polixenes, and with it that of the winter's tragedy falls on Florizel as the fullness and brightness of his poetry fades and diminishes into a shadowy abstraction where images are almost smothered at birth. This kind of writing is rare in the pastoral, but it is common in the tragic portion, particularly in Acts II and III. Thus Leontes:

> Camillo's flight,
> Added to their familiarity
> Which was as gross as ever touch'd conjecture,
> That lack'd sight only, nought for approbation
> But only seeing, all other circumstances
> Made up to the deed, doth push on this proceeding:
> Yet, for a greater confirmation...

Latinisms and abstractions have ousted the concrete Saxon words with which Shakespeare normally opposes them, though it might be difficult to find another six consecutive lines ending in Latin polysyllables. It would be equally difficult to find many lines like Hermione's 'My life stands in the level of your dreams', a line that is rhetorically and aesthetically complete in itself. Hermione opens her defence,

> Since what I am to say must be but that
> Which contradicts my accusation, and
> The testimony on my part no other
> But what comes from myself, it shall scarce boot me
> To say 'not guilty'.

Here the bleakness of the diction is emphasized by the free use of light and weak endings – *that, and* – completely breaking down the architectural form of the verse by

ROMANCES

sweeping one line into another without any definition of pause. This is made clearer if the speech is printed as prose:

> Since what I am to say must be but that which contradicts my accusation, and the testimony on my part no other but what comes from myself, it shall scarce boot me to say 'not guilty'.

It is a good example of Shakespeare's final sculptural form, but it is the form without the substance, the carving of a shadow; admirable for the neutral colloquial style that makes the transition from prose to verse almost imperceptible, but less admirable where the situation calls for poetry. Of course, it is not true to say that all, or even the greater part of the verse in the tragic scenes is as abstract and colourless as these passages; they are extreme examples, and the beginning of Mamillius' winter's tale about the man who dwelt by a churchyard is one of the most perfect things that Shakespeare ever did; but it is true that this bare latinized style, fluid in form, yet crabbed in expression, is sufficiently common to give *The Winter's Tale* a quality all its own.

What *Antony and Cleopatra* is to *Coriolanus*, *The Tempest* is to *The Winter's Tale* – the perfection of a dramatic form. *Pericles* fails in its first two acts, which, in addition to being mutilated in transmission, are the episodes of inconsequent romance, with little bearing on the main action of the play; *Cymbeline* collapses amid the complexities of its protracted *dénouement*; *The Winter's Tale* is broken-backed, for though Time as Chorus contrives to span the years, he cannot bridge the gulf between the tragedy and the romance. But in *The Tempest*, Shakespeare, with a backward glance at *The Comedy of Errors*, reduces the years between Miranda's birth and her maturity to a few lines of narrative, so concentrating the action within four hours, and confining it

235

to a single place. Then, with another backward glance, this time at *A Midsummer Night's Dream*, he solves the problem common to all these romances, their inherent and sometimes distracting improbability. *Pericles* and *The Winter's Tale* are fairy stories without the fairies, but by extending a doubtful probability to a patent impossibility even the impossible is made to appear probable. Once we have accepted the initial impossibility of Prospero's magic all things become probable, there is no further strain on our credulity, and Ariel, Caliban, the masque and the rest of the supernatural events follow almost as a matter of course. There is a corresponding perfection of theme. Instead of a commonplace story of misunderstandings and recognitions, and the eventual restoration of a heroine to her father, there is the much profounder conception of the restoration of all men to themselves when no man was his own. Then there is a further refinement: the discord in the minds of Alonso and his followers is symbolized by the tempest, their restoration by the music that allays its fury, their redemption by the harmony that resolves its noise. Allegory is a tiresome device in drama, and this is probably Shakespeare's only conscious employment of it; here, however, it is not a distracting parallel to be followed out of the corner of the mind's eye, but an element so woven into the play as to become an inseparable part.

Exquisite as the theme is, it is comparatively slight, and *The Tempest* has neither the sublimity nor the splendour of the great tragedies, but, as Prospero summons all the ministers of his magic for the final trial of his strength, so Shakespeare calls upon all the resources of his art to make his last play a worthy consummation of his life's work, and for sheer beauty, above all for the beauty of its poetry, it is unsurpassed. Not for the perfection of single lines is the poetry remarkable, for the later the play the less important

ROMANCES

is the line as a melodic unit – though there are lines as lovely as any that Shakespeare ever wrote: 'Sit still, and hear the last of our sea-sorrow', 'In the dark backward and abysm of time' – but for the phrase perfected by its relationship to the speech or the episode as a whole. In *The Winter's Tale* the verse of *Antony and Cleopatra* had been carried a stage further in the direction of fluidity, but it was bleached and drained of much of its colour; in *The Tempest* the colour is restored and the Shakespearean counterpoint completed.

There is no need to select a passage to illustrate this; the first verse speech in the play will do almost as well as any other. Miranda is watching the ship split on the rocks of the island:[3]

> If by your art, my dearest father, you have
> Put the wild waters in this roar, allay them.
> The sky, it seems, would pour down stinking pitch,
> But that the sea, mounting to the welkin's cheek,
> Dashes the fire out. O, I have suffer'd
> With those that I saw suffer! a brave vessel,
> Who had, no doubt, some noble creature in her,
> Dash'd all to pieces. O, the cry did knock
> Against my very heart. Poor souls, they perish'd.
> Had I been any god of power, I would
> Have sunk the sea within the earth, or e'er
> It should the good ship so have swallow'd, and
> The fraughting souls within her.

Instead of the pallid abstractions of Leontes and Hermione, here is the graphic immediacy that we associate with Shakespeare's poetry – the sea, a ship, and a cry – and here the visual quality of the verse is intensified by its free sculptural form, the contours of which both follow and direct the outline of the narrative. It is as though

The Poetry of Shakespeare's Plays

Shakespeare, conceiving the speech as a whole, took the words and modelled them into shape; by varying the position of the pauses and by kneading one line into another with a word so lightly stressed that the junction is not marked – 'you *have* put', 'would *have* sunk', swallow'd, *and* the fraughting souls' – he imposes a speech unit of any length on the limited one of the line, something in the same way that he sets up a counter-rhythm by means of the extra syllables of the feminine endings – 'dearest father, you have'. By concealing the linear structure, by infinite variations of the metrical pattern, and by the rejection of rhetorical artifice, Shakespeare has evolved a dramatic poetry with a rhythm that can be relaxed at will to approximate to that of prose, or tautened into the strictest formality of verse.

It is worth reminding ourselves at this stage that the origin of this protean verse is the wooden measure of *The Comedy of Errors*:

> For ere the ships could meet by twice five leagues,
> We were encounter'd by a mighty rock,
> Which being violently borne upon,
> Our helpful ship was splitted in the midst.

And even the king's splendid picture of the storm in 2 *Henry IV* appears elementary when compared with Miranda's:

> Wilt though upon the high and giddy mast
> Seal up the ship-boy's eyes, and rock his brains
> In cradle of the rude imperious surge,
> And in the visitation of the winds,
> Who take the ruffian billows by the top,
> Curling their monstrous heads, and hanging them
> With deafening clamour in the slippery clouds,
> That with the hurly death itself awakes?

ROMANCES

There is a further development in this late poetry. As the feminine ending is a vital element in Shakespeare's rhythm, and a reversal of the beat most forcibly suggested by a verbal trochee, it follows that the characteristic redundant syllable is always that of a trochaic word; monosyllabic feminine endings are rare before the poetry of the last phase, but in *The Tempest* there is a pronounced increase in their number, generally pronouns. Miranda's speech contains examples of both types – *suffer'd, vessel, perish'd; you have, allay them, in her* – the construction being repeated before the mid-line pauses – *suffer, pieces, within her*. This variation affords a further opportunity for refinement, and how beautifully the redundant monosyllable could be employed as illustrated in Prospero's speech,

> the very rats
> Instinctively have quit it: there they hoist us,
> To cry to the sea that roar'd to us; to sigh
> To the winds, whose pity, sighing back again,
> Did us but loving wrong.

The apparent reversal of the rhythm in *hoist us, quit it* is reinforced by the real reversal of *Did us*, varied in the regular *to us*, and by the rhyme *quit it – pity* all are incorporated in the exquisite music of the rising 'to cry to the sea... to sigh to the winds' and the falling 'sighing back again'.

'The isle is full of noises, sounds and sweet airs that give delight', says Caliban, and when we think of *The Tempest* it is music that we hear; not the heavenly music at Prospero's command, not even so much the songs of Ariel, as the music equally celestial of Shakespeare's latest blank verse spoken on that magic island more than three centuries ago: 'at midnight to fetch dew from the still-vex'd Bermoothes', 'with a charm join'd to their suffer'd labour', 'This music crept by me upon the waters', 'No wonder, sir, but certainly a maid', 'She that is queen of Tunis, she that dwells ten leagues beyond man's life', 'Sometimes a thousand twangling instruments will hum about mine ears', 'I'll seek him deeper than e'er plummet sounded', 'O brave new world, that has such people in't!' And then there is the poetry of Prospero.

'The character of the man is best seen in his writings', wrote Nicholas Rowe of Shakespeare a century after his death. But it is not so; his genius, of course, but not his character. Shakespeare was neither propagandist nor satirist; he did not write plays with a purpose and make a mouthpiece of his own creations; his characters are so real precisely because they are so completely detached from himself, and then again, his range is so immense, from Dogberry to Lear, from Lady Macbeth to Miranda, that we can very rarely be certain that any utterance is his own, and it is ironical that the man about whom of all men we should like to know most, because of his transcendent genius, is obscured by the genius itself. Yet there are three occasions on which we seem to hear his voice and catch a shadowy glimpse of the man: in some of the *Sonnets*, in *Hamlet*, and in *The Tempest*, written respectively at the beginning, in the middle, and at the end of his career. It was the poet Campbell who first identified Shakespeare with Prospero, and there is nothing over-fanciful in the idea that he should give himself the grand, confident poetry of the central character in his last and most beautiful play. More than that, it would have been most fitting had he himself played Prospero at the Globe theatre production which must have preceded that at Court in November 1611; although there is no record of his acting after 1603, he might well, like Othello, have said farewell to his occupation, and to the wooden O that he had immortalized in the dozen years that had passed since first he greeted it in *Henry V*. It may be, therefore, that Prospero's breaking of his staff and drowning of his book are symbolic of Shakespeare's retirement from the theatre:

> the strong-based promontory
> Have I made shake, and by the spurs pluck'd up
> The pine and cedar: graves at my command
> Have waked their sleepers, oped, and let 'em forth
> By my so potent art. But this rough magic
> I here abjure; and when I have required
> Some heavenly music – which even now I do –
> To work mine end upon their senses, that
> This airy charm is for, I'll break my staff,
> Bury it certain fathoms in the earth,
> And deeper than did ever plummet sound
> I'll drown my book.

The whole of this great speech, beginning 'Ye elves of hills', is a perfect example of what was said above, that the full beauty of a phrase is dependent on the passage as a whole, for each phrase is only a part of the Shakespearean counterpoint. Thus, almost every word in the last line and a half, with its powerfully retarded plunging movement, is the climax of a whole sequence of words that have preceded it – *cedar, sleepers, deeper; puppet, pluck'd up, plummet* – and the skilled reader of Shakespeare's poetry will look instinctively at the words at the end of a line and before a mid-line pause for the key to these harmonies.

All is reconciliation and restoration: Prospero to his dukedom, Ferdinand to his father, the sleeping sailors to their ship, Caliban to his island, and Ariel to the elements. Prospero has already given Miranda to Ferdinand, and with her that for which he lives, yet one feels that the pang of parting from Ariel was even greater. 'Why, that's my dainty Ariel! I shall miss thee', he says as Ariel helps to attire him and sings his last song in anticipation of freedom, and in no other play are the last words so moving as those of Prospero's echoing *Ariel – fare thou well*:

>   My Ariel, chick,
> That is thy charge: then to the elements
> Be free, and fare thou well!

---

1 See page 77.
2 Coleridge thought an epithet was wanted, 'for the balance, for the aesthetic logic. Perhaps "golden" was the word which would set off the "violets dim".' Surely not! Coleridge was remembering his Wordsworth.
3 As a good example of Shakespeare's range, compare this with the Clown's prose description of an identical scene in *The Winter's Tale*, III. iii.

Part Seven

EPILOGUE

Henry VIII, The Two Noble Kinsmen.

Shakespeare had already retired to Stratford when he wrote *The Tempest*, but he still paid occasional visits to London; he was there, for example, in the early summer of 1612 as a witness in a lawsuit, and again in March of the following year when he bought a house near the Blackfriars theatre. It was at about this time that Francis Beaumont married a wealthy heiress and threw up his career as dramatist, an event that would be a severe blow to his friend and partner John Fletcher, and something like a disaster to the King's Men, who had already lost Shakespeare. There can be little doubt, therefore, that Heminge and Condell and the rest of the company would appeal to Shakespeare to help them out of their difficulty by writing for them again, at least in collaboration with Fletcher, who would be responsible for the completion of the plays and relieve him of the trouble of putting them together and preparing them for performance. Shakespeare was not the sort of man to leave his friends and old colleagues in the lurch, and in collaboration with Fletcher wrote three plays: *Cardenio*, a romance that has been lost, *The Two Noble Kinsmen*, and *Henry VIII*, during one of the first performances of which, on 29 June 1613, the Globe was burned to the ground.

Although *Henry VIII* was published in the Folio as Shakespeare's work, and there is no external evidence of Fletcher's hand, or even of divided authorship, the fact that Fletcher is recorded as joint author with Shakespeare of *Cardenio* and *The Two Noble Kinsmen*, combined with the internal evidence of style, makes it almost certain that he

The Poetry of Shakespeare's Plays

was responsible for more than half of the play. If we read the following speeches, Wolsey's soliloquy on Anne Bullen in the first half of III. ii and that on his own downfall in the second half, we shall find it difficult to believe that the man who had recently written *The Tempest* wrote them both:

> What though I know her virtuous
> And well deserving? yet I know her for
> A spleeny Lutheran, and not wholesome to
> Our cause, that she should lie i' the bosom of
> Our hard-ruled king. Again there is sprung up
> An heretic, an arch one, Cranmer, one
> Hath crawl'd into the favour of the king,
> And is his oracle.

> Vain pomp and glory of this world, I hate ye:
> I feel my heart new open'd. O, how wretched
> Is that poor man that hangs on princes' favours!
> There is, betwixt that smile we would aspire to,
> That sweet aspect of princes, and their ruin,
> More pangs and fears than wars or women have:
> And when he falls, he falls like Lucifer,
> Never to hope again.

It seems quite clear that there are two styles: the first, Shakespeare's of the final period, with its predominantly masculine termination of line and frequent overflows emphasized by light and weak endings; the second, another's whose characteristic line is stopped with a feminine ending. It is true that one of the main elements in Shakespeare's latest poetry, indeed one of its greatest beauties, is the falling cadence of the feminine ending, but it is never overworked, and is only one of many devices — the real reversal of feet, and the apparent reversal induced by mid-foot pauses and by

EPILOGUE

assonance – that give a similar rhythmical effect *anywhere within the line*, and these, in conjunction with run-on lines and the constant variation of the strength and position of the pause, produce a vital and muscular rhythm that is capable of any degree of tension and any modification of speed. Such a rhythm, however, could not be claimed for those parts of *Henry VIII* in which Fletcher's hand is suspected. Nearly all the lines are built on the same pattern: five regular iambic feet followed by a redundant syllable, often a stressed monosyllabic pronoun, and a well-defined pause. Strong pauses within the line are rare, but there is often a short one before, in the middle of, or after the fourth foot, leaving a unit of three to five syllables at the end of the line: 'I hate ye', 'O, how wretched'. Though single lines are often exceedingly beautiful, in a long speech the regularity of the falling cadence becomes maddeningly monotonous.

Now compare the second style with that of a speech from *Valentinian*, a tragedy written by Fletcher at about the same time as *Henry VIII*:

> Get ye from me!
> Is not the doom of Caesar on this body?
> Do not I bear my last hour here, now sent me?
> Am I not old Aecius, ever dying?
> You think this tenderness and love you bring me;
> 'Tis treason, and the strength of disobedience,
> And, if ye tempt me further, ye shall feel it.

The same mannerisms are here, the mannerisms that make the drooping rhythms, the languishing cadences, the exhausted and enervated verse of Fletcher. For certain effects, particularly for the exploitation of the pathetic, Fletcher's verse is admirable, and he was a poet of more than common merit, but he was not a great dramatic poet, and a whole play by him is cloying in its over-sweet monotony. He was a born collaborator who could turn an exquisite lyric and was excellent at a speech or a scene of distress, and that is why in *Henry VIII* Shakespeare broaches the main themes and introduces the characters, Buckingham, Wolsey, Katharine, leaving them to be killed off by Fletcher. For *Henry VIII* is barely a play; it is a series of loosely related private disasters interspersed with pageants, so that at the end, apart from the king himself, we are left with a set of characters quite different from those at the beginning. Nor is the poetry of a very high order, for the scenes that lend themselves to the greatest poetry, scenes that would have been very differently developed by Shakespeare, were written by Fletcher.

In a sense Fletcher was unfortunate in his collaborator. It was one thing to have as partner a man like Beaumont whose ability was similar to his own, but quite another to set his work beside that of the most experienced dramatist of his age and the greatest poet of all time. His own contribution was bound to suffer by the comparison, and in judging it we must make allowance for this and then ask ourselves what other man could have come off so creditably. Yet in the seventeenth century Fletcher's plays were more popular than Shakespeare's, and even today any popularity that *Henry VIII* may be said to possess lies in Fletcher's pageantry and the protracted farewells of Henry's victims. Admittedly, if we take a few lines from one of these speeches they are very moving:

> And when I am forgotten, as I shall be,
> And sleep in dull cold marble, where no mention
> Of me more must be heard of, say, I taught thee;
> Say, Wolsey, that once trod the ways of glory,
> And sounded all the depths and shoals of honour,

EPILOGUE

Found thee a way, out of his wreck, to rise in;
A sure and safe one, though thy master miss'd it.

But these are only seven lines out of a very long farewell indeed, longer even than Buckingham's, and how fresh and vigorous Shakespeare's introductory verse sounds in comparison:

The king in this perceives him, how he coasts
And hedges his own way. But in this point
All his tricks founder, and he brings his physic
After his patient's death.

'The genius of Shakespeare comes in and goes out with Katharine', wrote Johnson, but it would be truer to say that Katharine comes in with the genius of Shakespeare and goes out with that of Fletcher. Hers is the third of Fletcher's farewells to life and greatness, a remarkable demonstration of his command of the pathetic, and dexterously he redeploys his apparatus, the flowers, the words of sorrowful connotation and the elegiac cadences, while Katharine is made all forgiveness and solicitude for her 'wenches', her 'wretched women' and 'poor people':

When I am dead, good wench,
Let me be used with honour: strew me over
With maiden flowers, that all the world may know
I was a chaste wife to my grave: embalm me,
Then lay me forth; although unqueen'd, yet like
A queen, and daughter to a king, inter me.

We can imagine how Fletcher must have itched to write the trial scene, and what he would have made of it. But Shakespeare never exploits the pathos inherent in the feminine ending; on the contrary, he always deliberately avoids its melancholy cadence in anguished scenes, disdaining to force the pity by illegitimate devices. So here, and the only talk of weeping is the beautiful,

> Sir,
> I am about to weep; but, thinking that
> We are a queen, or long have dream'd so, certain
> The daughter of a king, my drops of tears
> I'll turn to sparks of fire.

The pattern of *Henry VIII* is repeated in *The Two Noble Kinsmen*, though with a difference. Shakespeare sets the play in motion and introduces the main characters, leaving the elaboration of the middle scenes to Fletcher, but then returns to write the final act. Fletcher is thus responsible for the ridiculous and revolting sub-plot of the jailer's distracted daughter, a theme and a treatment that are as characteristic of him as they are foreign to Shakespeare, and the difference between the two is much more marked than in *Henry VIII*, Fletcher rarely rising above the level of a smutty and sentimental mediocrity, while Shakespeare writes some of his noblest poetry, in particular Arcite's invocation to Mars in the last act:

> Though mighty one, that with thy power hast turn'd
> Green Neptune into purple; whose approach
> Comets prewarn; whose havoc in vast fields
> Unearthed skulls proclaim; whose breath blows down
> The teeming Ceres' foison; who dost pluck
> With hand armipotent from forth blue clouds
> The mason'd turrets...

Epilogue

As far as we know, the lines with which Theseus concludes *The Two Noble Kinsmen* are the last that we possess by Shakespeare, and they are not inappropriate as a valediction:

> O, you heavenly charmers,
> What things you make of us! For what we lack
> We laugh, for what we have, are sorry still,
> Are children in some kind. Let us be thankful
> For that which is, and with you leave dispute
> That are above our question. Let's go off,
> And bear us like the time.

The Epilogue is Fletcher's, but the last words are spoken on behalf of Shakespeare as well: 'Gentlemen, good night.'

F E Halliday

Shakespeare in His Age

The life and work of Shakespeare is put into context in this fascinating volume, based on the assertion that in order to understand this great writer, we must appreciate the epoch in which he existed. Beginning with a description of the England into which he was born, his political and cultural inheritance, each year of his half-century lifetime is meticulously charted, noting the forces that helped to determine his development and his work.

'This admirable book covers a vast amount of ground with fluency and depth' *The Spectator*

'Once more Mr Halliday produces a work which can be classed where his *Shakespeare Companion* stands already…this time he offers a copious description of Shakespeare's times and all the variety of English life and action which surround him' *The Times*

The Life of Shakespeare

The most prolific scholar of William Shakespeare's life and work fills in the gaps between the beads of biographical fact with a more than satisfying degree of probability. Halliday traces Shakespeare's movements during the most important years of his life, discussing the theatrical, political and social pressures to which he was subject.

'A quick-moving and workmanlike biography…admirably compact and comprehensive…clear and energetic prose' *Observer*

F E Halliday

A History of Cornwall

This classic history of Cornwall provides a comprehensive review of Britain's most south-westerly county.

With absorbing detail, Halliday relates the story of the Bronze Age stone circles and Iron Age citadels; the coming of the Saints; the dissolution of the monasteries and the Tudor rebellions; the Armada and the war with Spain; the preaching of John Wesley; the making of the railway; and into this fascinating pattern of the centuries he weaves the two threads of the sea and Cornish tin.

In this clear and vibrant account, Halliday skilfully illustrates what makes this historic county so exceptional.

Wordsworth and His World

William Wordsworth, born in 1770, was the eldest and possibly the greatest member of the English Romantic movement. The English countryside was his chief inspiration – in so much of his work he combined a passionate apprehension of nature with a belief that nature is the source of man's innate goodness. He was determined to express his ideals in terms of the lives of ordinary people, and using the plainest language, which caused a revolution in English poetic style – though his verse rises to heights of splendour, which few other English poets can match.

Halliday's biography turns a mighty name into a human being.

F E Halliday

Thomas Hardy: His Life and Work

Hardy's belief that 'The ultimate aim of the poet should be to touch our hearts by showing his own,' is endorsed in his own works – whether poetry or prose, his compassion is what lends it greatness. The full appreciation of his work depends on an understanding of his life: they are so inextricably intertwined that they must be treated together.

With the refined estimation of an expert, Halliday gives us a remarkable introduction to Hardy's anguished soul and brilliant work.

'F E Halliday has produced, with practised skill, an admirable short life...the book is a model of accurate information' *Times Literary Supplement*

Doctor Johnson and His World

Written with a deep and sympathetic knowledge of Johnson's life and works, Halliday's biography takes a close look at what Johnson's peers wrote about him, and what he himself wrote during his lifetime; including his *Dictionary*, which was a major step forward in lexicography, and his *Lives of the Poets*, which remain models of sound literary judgement. The book is set in the context of the dazzling social circle in which Dr Johnson moved, which included Garrick, Sir Joshua Reynolds, Goldsmith, Burke and Fanny Burney.

TITLES BY F E HALLIDAY AVAILABLE DIRECT FROM HOUSE OF STRATUS

Quantity		£	$(US)	$(CAN)	€
☐	Chaucer and His World	8.99	13.95	20.95	15.00
☐	Doctor Johnson and His World	8.99	13.95	20.95	15.00
☐	A History of Cornwall	10.99	16.95	25.95	18.00
☐	The Life of Shakespeare	10.99	16.95	25.95	18.00
☐	Robert Browning: His Life and Work	9.99	14.95	22.95	16.50
☐	Shakespeare and His Critics	8.99	13.95	20.95	15.00
☐	A Shakespeare Companion	14.99	22.95	34.95	25.00
☐	Shakespeare in His Age	10.99	16.95	25.95	18.00
☐	Thomas Hardy: His Life and Work	10.99	16.95	25.95	18.00
☐	Unfamiliar Shakespeare	10.99	16.95	25.95	18.00
☐	Wordsworth and His World	8.99	13.95	20.95	15.00

ALL HOUSE OF STRATUS BOOKS ARE AVAILABLE FROM GOOD BOOKSHOPS OR DIRECT FROM THE PUBLISHER:

Internet: www.houseofstratus.com including synopses and features.

Email: sales@houseofstratus.com please quote author, title and credit card details.

Order Line:
UK: 0800 169 1780,
USA: 1 800 509 9942
INTERNATIONAL: +44 (0) 20 7494 6400 (UK)
or +01 212 218 7649
(please quote author, title, and credit card details.)

Send to:
House of Stratus Sales Department
24c Old Burlington Street
London
W1X 1RL
UK

House of Stratus Inc.
Suite 210
1270 Avenue of the Americas
New York • NY 10020
USA

PAYMENT

Please tick currency you wish to use:

☐ £ (Sterling)   ☐ $ (US)   ☐ $ (CAN)   ☐ € (Euros)

Allow for shipping costs charged per order plus an amount per book as set out in the tables below:

CURRENCY/DESTINATION	£(Sterling)	$(US)	$(CAN)	€ (Euros)
Cost per order				
UK	1.50	2.25	3.50	2.50
Europe	3.00	4.50	6.75	5.00
North America	3.00	3.50	5.25	5.00
Rest of World	3.00	4.50	6.75	5.00
Additional cost per book				
UK	0.50	0.75	1.15	0.85
Europe	1.00	1.50	2.25	1.70
North America	1.00	1.00	1.50	1.70
Rest of World	1.50	2.25	3.50	3.00

PLEASE SEND CHEQUE OR INTERNATIONAL MONEY ORDER.
payable to: STRATUS HOLDINGS plc or HOUSE OF STRATUS INC. or card payment as indicated

STERLING EXAMPLE

Cost of book(s):. . . . . Example: 3 x books at £6.99 each: £20.97

Cost of order:. . . . . Example: £1.50 (Delivery to UK address)

Additional cost per book:. . . . . Example: 3 x £0.50: £1.50

Order total including shipping:. Example: £23.97

VISA, MASTERCARD, SWITCH, AMEX:

☐☐☐☐ ☐☐☐☐ ☐☐☐☐ ☐☐☐☐

Issue number (Switch only):

☐☐☐

Start Date: Expiry Date:

☐☐/☐☐   ☐☐/☐☐

Signature: _____

NAME: _____

ADDRESS: _____

COUNTRY: _____

ZIP/POSTCODE: _____

Please allow 28 days for delivery. Despatch normally within 48 hours.

Prices subject to change without notice.
Please tick box if you do not wish to receive any additional information. ☐

House of Stratus publishes many other titles in this genre; please check our website (www.houseofstratus.com) for more details.